THE GREATEST
★ SPORTS TEAM ★
RIVALRIES

THE GREATEST ★ SPORTS TEAM ★ RIVALRIES

By MATT CHRISTOPHER®

THE #1 SPORTS SERIES FOR KIDS

LITTLE, BROWN AND COMPANY
NEW YORK • BOSTON

Little, Brown and Company

Hachette Book Group
237 Park Avenue, New York, NY 10017
Visit our website at www.lb-kids.com

www.mattchristopher.com

Little, Brown and Company is a division of Hachette Book Group, Inc. The Little, Brown name and logo are trademarks of Hachette Book Group, Inc.

The publisher is not responsible for websites (or their content) that are not owned by the publisher.

First Edition: January 2012

Matt Christopher® is a registered trademark of Matt Christopher Royalties, Inc.

Text written by Stephanie True Peters

Library of Congress Cataloging-in-Publication Data

Christopher, Matt.
The greatest sports team rivalries / Matt Christopher ; [text by Stephanie True Peters].—1st ed.
p. cm.—(The #1 sports series for kids)
Summary: "Competition is the name of the game in sports. But without a doubt, the fiercest battles are fought when longtime rivals come face-to-face. Here are in-depth looks at five such legendary rivalries: the Yankees versus the Red Sox, the Celtics versus the Lakers, the United versus the Galaxy, the Canadiens versus the Bruins, and the Bears versus the Packers. Each section is packed with intense play-by-play game action, recaps of classic moments that sparked the feuds, and insights into heated clashes."—Provided by publisher.
ISBN 978-0-316-17687-3
1. Sports rivalries—United States—History—Juvenile literature. I. Peters, Stephanie True, 1965– II. Title.
GV583.C475 2012
796.0973—dc23

2011019226

10 9 8 7 6 5 4 3 2 1

CW

Printed in the United States of America

Contents

Chapter One
The New York Yankees versus the Boston Red Sox   1

Chapter Two
The Boston Celtics versus the Los Angeles Lakers   31

Chapter Three
D.C. United versus the Los Angeles Galaxy   58

Chapter Four
The Montreal Canadiens versus the Boston Bruins   84

Chapter Five
The Chicago Bears versus the Green Bay Packers   107

Appendix
Rivalry Roundup!   127

THE GREATEST
★ SPORTS TEAM ★
RIVALRIES

★ CHAPTER ONE ★

The New York Yankees
versus the Boston Red Sox

The Boston Red Sox were in trouble. The regular season was coming to a close, and they were too far behind in the standings to make the playoffs. The players were frustrated, and their fans were disappointed. So was the club's owner, Harry H. Frazee. Losing franchises don't bring in profits, and he was already on shaky financial ground. So when the New York Yankees offered him a huge sum of cash for one of his players, he took it.

With that sale, a rivalry that had been simmering for years exploded into the most intense and longest-lived feud in all of American sports: the Boston Red Sox versus the New York Yankees. What player could possibly cause such a rift? None other than Babe Ruth.

George Herman "Babe" Ruth's trade in 1919

turned up the heat in this rivalry, but it didn't cause it. The cities of Boston and New York had a history of jealousy and hatred that began long before Ruth or professional baseball even existed. Boston was once the most important city in the Northeast, until New York's economy took off in the 1700s. Soon, New York had grown into a booming metropolis that surpassed Boston in size and significance. Boston resented being overshadowed as much as New York enjoyed its new global importance, and so any harmonious relationship they might have shared disappeared.

Given the competitive nature of sports, it's no surprise that the cities' animosity spilled over into baseball. When the American League formed in 1901, Boston's club, then called the Americans, was one of its first members. The New York Highlanders, as the Yankees were first known, started out as a minor-league team in Baltimore before moving to New York and joining the league in 1903. The teams played their first official American League game on May 7 that year. Boston won 6–2. They won twelve of their following nineteen matches with New York, too—and ended the sea-

son by winning the first World Series championship.

Boston was the victor in the first Yankees–Red
Sox pennant race as well. Throughout September
of 1904, Boston and New York traded first place
back and forth. There was no World Series that
year because of ongoing animosity between the
American and National Leagues. Without that
championship, the pennant race took on even
greater meaning for the league leaders.

The Yankees took Game One of the best-of-five
series. Then the teams traveled to Boston for a doubleheader. Much to the delight of the thirty thousand
rabid hometown fans in attendance, the Sox crushed
the Yankees in their first outing that day 13–2.

Boston's fans might have played a part in the
lopsided win. A large group of them watched the
game from behind a roped-off area in the outfield.
Any ball hit into that crowd was an automatic double. According to Red Sox lore, when Boston hit
one in their direction, the fans moved the rope forward. When New York threatened, they moved it
back!

The Sox won the third game, too, though by a

much slimmer margin of just 1–0. They took the fourth in the series as well, although they might not have if not for Yankees pitcher "Happy Jack" Chesbro (an ironic nickname, considering his scowl). Chesbro usually threw with pinpoint accuracy, but in the top of the ninth inning with a runner on third, he hurled a wild pitch. Boston scored the go-ahead run and, after holding off the Yankees in the bottom of the ninth, took the game 3–2. That victory sealed their first-place spot; New York took the fifth match 1–0, but it was too little, too late. The Red Sox were the 1904 American League champions.

A decade later, Babe Ruth made his professional debut with the Red Sox. In the next five years as a pitcher and outfielder for Boston, the Bambino baffled batters and foiled runners with his cannon of an arm. In 1916, he had a league-best earned run average (ERA) of 1.75 and the greatest number of shutouts with nine. Three years later, unparalleled at bat, he led the league in runs (103), home runs (29), and runs batted in (114), among other stats. With Ruth in the lineup, the Red Sox won three World Series in four years.

And then Harry Frazee sold him to the Yankees.

Losing Ruth was a bitter disappointment to the Sox. Losing Ruth to New York was an absolute outrage. Frazee quickly became one of the most hated men in Boston. How upset were fans? According to one story, years after the trade, Frazee was taking a cab to Fenway Park, Boston's ball field. When the driver, a die-hard Red Sox follower, figured out who his rider was, he punched Frazee in the face!

From the moment Ruth pulled on the pinstriped uniform of the Yankees, he was a legend in New York. He laced his first New York home run on May 1, 1920—against the Red Sox. He tallied an unbelievable fifty-three additional four-baggers that same season, thirty-five more homers than the next best hitter. He and his powerful bat led the team to back-to-back-to-back American League championships in 1921, 1922, and 1923.

As Ruth's fame grew, so did the Yankees' wealth, for fans flocked to games to see the Sultan of Swat hit home runs. In 1923, that money enabled the team to build Yankee Stadium, known forever after as The House That Ruth Built. It also allowed them to stack their roster with some of the league's best players. To the fury of Boston, many of those players came from the Red Sox lineup. Those players included Ernie Shore, who once noted that New York in those years "was the Red Sox dynasty in Yankee uniforms."

With that high-powered roster plus rookie sensation Lou Gehrig slotted in the lineup, Ruth and the Yankees won their first World Series in 1923. That first title was followed by a second in 1927, the year Ruth blasted sixty homers, more than any other team total combined. The Yankees were outstanding that season, winning 110 games and losing only forty-four to earn the nickname "Murderers' Row" for the way they destroyed opponents. A third championship came in 1928, and a fourth in 1932.

Even after Ruth signed as a free agent with the Boston Braves in 1935—he was forty years old then and in failing health—the Yankees continued their meteoric rise to the top with four more World Series victories in 1936, 1937, 1938, and 1939. Boston, meanwhile, wallowed in the cellar season after season. With one team so much less competitive, the rivalry seemed to be dead.

But in reality, it was very much alive in the hearts

of the players, the coaches, and the fans—as an incident on May 30, 1938, proved.

The Red Sox had a strong start that season with nineteen wins and fourteen losses. The Yankees were equally good and had a record of 17–14 going into the first game of a doubleheader. Expecting to see one of the best matchups of the season, an estimated 83,500 fans packed into Yankee Stadium.

New York claimed an 8–0 lead by the bottom of the fourth inning. On the mound for the Red Sox was relief pitcher Archie McKain. Perhaps McKain was frustrated by the uneven score, for he nearly hit batter Jake Powell with one pitch—and then did hit him with another!

Infuriated, Powell charged the mound. That brought Boston's player-manager Joe Cronin rushing onto the field. In one motion, Cronin yanked Powell off McKain and slugged the Yankee! Other players and the umpires broke up the fight, Cronin and Powell were ejected, and the game resumed.

But so did the fight. On his way to the clubhouse, Cronin found Powell and several other Yankees waiting for him. Taunts turned into punches in a matter of seconds. The brawl was in full swing under the stands when umpires noticed the New York dugout was suspiciously empty, and they intervened.

The 1938 Cronin-Powell melee did much to reignite the hatred between the Yankees and the Red Sox. But it was a decades-long rivalry between two of the greatest hitters in the history of the sport that kept that anger burning hot.

Joe DiMaggio had debuted with the Yankees in May 1936. An outfielder whose speed had earned him the nickname "Yankee Clipper," after a new airplane, he hit twenty-nine homers and 125 runs batted in (RBIs), and scored 132 runs in his rookie season. His talking bat helped the Yankees regain their number-one ranking that year and to win the first of four consecutive World Series rings. While not the home-run king Babe Ruth had once been, DiMaggio was nearly unparalleled at the plate at that time.

Then Ted Williams came along. Boston had slowly emerged from its slump to reach second place in 1938, thanks in large part to slugger Jimmie Foxx. But the Sox needed a second strong hitter. They got one in Williams. In his rookie year in 1939, he logged the most RBIs with 145; the next season, he had the highest run total with 134. As good as he was in those years, they were nothing compared with his batting accomplishments in 1941.

Going into the Red Sox's final doubleheader of the regular season, Williams had a batting average of .3996. If he had chosen not to play either game that day, that number would have been rounded up to .400 in the record books. But Williams wanted to earn that .400 honestly. So, knowing he could ruin his average as easily as he could increase it, he played in both—and went six for eight at the plate to finish the season with an amazing batting average of .406!

Williams would probably have been the toast of the majors that year if not for DiMaggio. On May 15, DiMaggio hit an RBI single in the first inning of a game against the Chicago White Sox. The hit was noteworthy because it scored the only Yankees run of the day. But otherwise, it was hardly re-markable.

What was remarkable was the fact that DiMaggio got another hit in his next game—and his next, and his next, and so on throughout June and into July! By his own admission, the pressure DiMaggio felt to keep the streak alive was immense. Still, when it came to an end July 17, he didn't feel relief, but sorrow—and perhaps, deep down, a bit of amazement at what he had done. And rightfully so: He had ninety-one hits in 223 at-bats from May 15 to July 16 for an average of .408. That feat and his strong stats in other categories earned him the American League Most Valuable Player (MVP) award, not to mention the undying admiration of his teammates and his fans.

Williams, who came in second in the MVP voting, offered cordial congratulations to his rival, while subtly reminding people of his own successful season. "It took the Big Guy to beat me," he said.

After 1941, Williams's and DiMaggio's names were forever linked as combatants for the Greatest Hitter title. Williams earned a Triple Crown in 1942, with the American League's best batting average (.356), greatest number of home runs (36), and most RBIs (137). Yet he lost the MVP award to DiMaggio's teammate Joe Gordon.

Joltin' Joe DiMaggio and the Splendid Splinter left baseball for the armed forces from 1943 to 1945. Williams picked up where he left off when he returned, earning his first MVP award in 1946 and helping his team win the pennant for the first time since 1918. Sadly for hopeful Boston fans, the Sox lost to the St. Louis Cardinals four games to three, but at least they'd beaten the third-place Yankees in the league standings.

The following year, the teams traded ranks, with Boston finishing third and New York taking the pennant—and the 1947 World Series. Williams posted his second Triple Crown with a batting average of .343, thirty-two home runs, and 114 RBIs, yet missed the MVP award by a single vote to DiMaggio. The Red Sox came close to reaching the World Series in 1948 but lost first place to the Cleveland Indians in a sudden-death playoff tiebreaker.

The 1949 regular season ended in a tie, too, when the Yankees and the Red Sox finished with identical records of ninety-six wins and fifty-seven losses. The single-game elimination was played October 2, with the winner advancing to the World Series. Williams got up to bat four times that day—and frustratingly for himself and his fans, he was walked twice. DiMaggio rapped out a triple in one of his four at-bats but died on base. Still, his team held back a last-inning surge by the Sox to take the win 5–3.

One week after the tiebreaker, the Yankees won their twelfth World Series. It was the start of a five-year streak of championship wins. DiMaggio retired in 1951 midway through that streak. In constant pain from injuries, he was frank about his reason for leaving. "I feel I have reached the stage where I can no longer produce for my ball club, my manager, my teammates, and my fans the sort of baseball their loyalty to me deserves," the three-time MVP said when he announced his retirement.

Williams played ball through the 1960 season. His career achievements were so spectacular that he may in fact have been what he'd always longed to be: the greatest hitter of all time. Yet, surprisingly, in a town that worshipped its baseball heroes, he was not a fan favorite in Boston. Their dislike stemmed from his refusal to acknowledge their cheers in the ballpark with the time-honored gesture of tipping his cap.

Still, if not for Williams, the Sox might never have challenged the Yankees as they did in the years he was on the roster, for no team was more dominant than New York. With star players Mickey Mantle and Roger Maris headlining the roster, the Yankees' string of World Series wins and appearances continued nearly unbroken from 1954 to 1964. Out of nine championships played that decade, they won four to bring their overall total to twenty.

Then the unexpected happened: The Yankees fell to sixth place in the American League in 1965 and tenth in 1966. The Red Sox weren't much better, finishing ninth both years. New York didn't improve much in the early months of the 1967 season. The Boston club, on the other hand, suddenly revived to begin its first serious run at the pennant in nearly twenty years.

On June 20, the Red Sox were closing in on third place when they felled New York 7–1 at Yankee Stadium. They started out strong the next day, too, with a three-run homer in the first inning to help them to a 4–0 lead.

There were some solid hits in the second inning,

too, but not by a bat on a ball. In the top of the inning, New York hurler Thad Tillotson threw a pitch that struck batter Joe Foy in the head. Boston returned the favor in the bottom of the second when pitcher Jim Lonborg socked Tillotson between the shoulder blades. That blast cleared the benches as angry teammates rushed the field and began throwing punches. The umpires eventually got things under control, and the Red Sox went on to win 8–1 to tie for third place.

Boston finished the 1967 season, dubbed the Impossible Dream by the media, in first place. The Red Sox faced the St. Louis Cardinals in Boston's first World Series appearance since 1946. But the Cards turned the dream into a nightmare in Game Seven by beating the Sox 7–2 in front of thirty-five thousand screaming Boston fans.

While neither Boston nor New York returned to the championship in the next few years, their regular-season meetings gave their fans plenty to rant and rave about. Lopsided scores, long-running matches, exciting player matchups, and sudden brawls fueled the rivalry between them throughout the late 1960s and early 1970s.

One on-field fight in particular demonstrated the rivalry's intensity. The game took place in Fenway Park on August 1, 1973. The score was tied 2–2 in the top of the ninth. Yankees catcher Thurman Munson stood on third with Felipe Alou on first. If Munson crossed the plate, New York would have the lead.

Unfortunately, batter Gene Michael missed the bunt intended to squeeze Munson safely home. Munson, already well on his way, kept going. He barreled into Boston's catcher, Carlton Fisk. Fisk had the ball in his glove, however, so Munson was out.

The play might have ended there if Munson had stood up and walked away. Instead, he stayed on top of Fisk to prevent Fisk from throwing Alou out at second. Infuriated at being held down, Fisk tossed Munson off. Munson retaliated by punching Fisk. The two grappled, and then Michael joined in. The brawl ended with Fisk and Munson being ejected; the Red Sox won 3–2 on an RBI single.

Fisk was at the heart of another slugfest three years later. On May 20, 1976, the Yankees were hosting the Red Sox. As usual, New York fans turned out in droves to "welcome" their rivals.

"There'd be a mob waiting for us," Fisk recalled of trips to Yankee Stadium. "They'd be screaming at us and spitting and throwing things."

In the bottom of the sixth inning, New York's Lou Piniella tried to reach home from second on a long hit to right field. But outfielder Dwight Evans caught the ball and hurled it to Fisk at the plate. In a replay of the Fisk-Munson altercation, Piniella bowled into Fisk, who threw him off and then hit him. Other players joined in the fracas, including Yankee Graig Nettles. Nettles got the worst of the fight with torn shoulder ligaments; New York got the worst of the game, losing 8–2 when Carl Yastrzemski hit homers in the eighth and ninth innings. But the Yankees had the last laugh, for when the season ended, they had the pennant while the Sox had third place.

The Yankees continued thumbing their nose at the Red Sox—and every other team—by winning a hundred games in 1977 and 1978. Two of those 1978 wins came in early September, when the Yankees were busy erasing Boston's lead of fourteen and a half games in the standings. The first game saw New York demolish the Red Sox 15–3. The Yankees then took the next day's match 13–2. This two-day Red Sox embarrassment was later nicknamed the Boston Massacre, but the Boston club's true demise came October 2.

The 1978 season had ended in a first-place tie between the Red Sox and the Yankees. The October 2 game was played to break that tie. Boston had a 2–0 advantage when New York came up to bat at the top of the seventh. The Red Sox collected an out but then allowed two singles to put runners on first and second. Pinch hitter Jim Spencer then flied out, bringing up Bucky Dent.

With just four home runs for the year, Dent was hardly a batting threat. And yet—*pow!*—he laced a homer that scored three runs to put the Yankees up by one! Two more runs scored for each team by the end of New York's at-bats. When Boston couldn't overcome the single-run deficit in the bottom of the ninth, the Yankees took the pennant—and, later, their second consecutive World Series.

That championship crowned the New York

Yankees as the undisputed ruling dynasty of Major League Baseball. But even the greatest teams in sports undergo slowdowns, and soon after the 1978 win, the Yankees fell into a slump that lasted several years. They returned to power in 1994, the year the World Series was canceled because of a players' strike, and stayed at or near the top for the next five seasons. Boston's place in the standings fluctuated year to year, with a first-place finish followed by a third-place disappointment for Sox fans. Then, in 1999, a long-hoped-for matchup finally occurred: The Red Sox and the Yankees met for the first time ever in the postseason.

The meeting came about because of changes to the structure of the playoffs. The American League had expanded into three divisions, East, Central, and West. At season's end, the top team from each division plus the best team of the number two divisional slots battled for the chance to advance to the league championship. In 1999, the Yankees were the best team in the American League East and Boston earned the fourth playoff slot. They both defeated their challengers in the Division Series matchups to face each other in the

American League Championship Series (ALCS), the winner of which would then advance to the World Series.

With their hometowns buzzing with excitement, New York and Boston played Game One to a 3–3 tie to send the match into extra innings. The Red Sox failed to score in their turn at bat. New York, however, got a walk-off home run from Bernie Williams in the bottom of the tenth to win 4–3. The Yankees won the next night, too, 3–2.

Game Three was a much-anticipated shoot-out between former Red Sox pitcher Roger Clemens and current Red Sox ace Pedro Martinez. Martinez and the Sox sent their old teammate packing after just two innings—and the Yankees back to the locker room with their tails between their legs with a 13–1 victory for Boston. New York returned the favor the next night, however, by crushing Boston 9–2.

The Yankees jumped to an early 2–0 lead in the first inning of the fifth game. They doubled that score in the seventh. The Red Sox managed to put one on the board with a home run by Jason Varitek in the bottom of the eighth. They threatened to jump ahead when, with the bases loaded and just one out, pinch hitter Scott Hatteberg struck out and Trot Nixon flied out. New York answered with two more runs in their last at-bat to make it 6–1. When the Sox couldn't produce in the bottom of the ninth, the Yankees were once more on their way to the World Series.

Martinez and Clemens dueled again in the ALCS four years later. Martinez made headlines in Game Three, though it wasn't for his pitching. In the fourth inning, the dugouts emptied when Clemens nearly hit Boston batter Manny Ramirez. For some reason, Yankees bench coach Don Zimmer targeted Martinez. Martinez responded by grabbing the seventy-two-year-old by the back of the head and throwing him to the ground.

Boston lost that game but stayed afloat in the next three to force a seventh match. That was as far as they went. Yankee Aaron Boone became a hero that night when he homered off pitcher Tim Wakefield in the eleventh inning to seal the victory for New York. The Red Sox's only satisfaction was watching the Yankees lose in the World Series to the Florida Marlins.

In 2004, the Red Sox suffered a loss to the Yankees even before the season began. Boston management had long had its eye on superstar Alex Rodriguez. Rodriguez was leaving the Texas Rangers and seemed interested in Boston. Unfortunately, talks broke down in December 2003—and two months later, A-Rod signed with the Yankees.

The Red Sox and Yankees had many classic duels throughout the 2004 season, including an extra-inning battle July 1 that featured Yankee shortstop Derek Jeter's leaping into the stands for a catch and emerging with the ball and a blood-streaked face. Three weeks later, tempers flared when A-Rod and Varitek mixed it up after Rodriguez was nearly hit by a pitch. Both players were ejected; Boston won the match.

Games and incidents like those kept the century-old rivalry smoldering throughout the season. But it was in the 2004 postseason that it burst into flames.

The Yankees were the best team in the American League, finishing with 101 wins and sixty-one losses. Boston was the second best with a 98–64 record. They both dispatched their opponents in the Division Series to set up an epic rematch in the ALCS.

The two storied franchises met for Game One on October 12 in Yankee Stadium. Fans expected to see a pitcher's duel between Red Sox ace Curt Schilling and New York's Mike Mussina. But it never materialized because Schilling was suffering from an injury to his right ankle that affected his pitching. The crowd was treated to an exciting match nonetheless, for the Sox surged from behind to draw within one at the top of the eighth. The Yankees held them off, however, and finished with a 10–7 win.

New York won Game Two before the hometown crowd as well—and then silenced Boston's faithful by demolishing the Sox 19–8. That humiliating defeat had even the most loyal Red Sox fans groaning. "Soon it will be over," predicted one Boston newspaper reporter, "and we will spend another dreary winter lamenting this and lamenting that."

But it wasn't over yet. The Yankees had to earn one more win to advance to the World Series.

They didn't get it the next match. That night, the

score was New York 4, Boston 3 going into the bottom of the ninth. Boston's Kevin Millar came up to bat. He was handed a walk by pitcher Mariano Rivera. Dave Roberts took Millar's place on first to pinch-run for him. And run he did, stealing second on Rivera's first pitch.

"That's why we have a guy like Dave Roberts," Boston outfielder Johnny Damon said. "He's one of the best base stealers around."

That base stealer crossed home plate one single later to tie the game and send it into extra innings. Three innings later—*pow!*—Boston slugger David Ortiz blasted a two-run homer. The Red Sox won 6–4 to stay alive in the series.

They won the next match as well, after a grueling fourteen innings and nearly six hours of play. Once again, Ortiz saved the day with a line drive to center field that sent Damon across home plate and broke the 4–4 tie.

To New York's shock, Boston took Game Six, too. Pitcher Curt Schilling was the hero that night. He had had surgery to temporarily help his injured ankle, but midway through the match, blood was clearly seeping through his sock. How bad was it?

"You ever walk in the rain in your socks? That's what it felt like," Schilling once said of playing in his now famous bloody sock.

After decades of disappointment, Boston fans— or Red Sox Nation, as they are known—finally allowed themselves to hope. Yankees fans stayed confident, however, for history was on their side.

Game Seven was played on October 20 in Yankee Stadium. More than fifty-six thousand fans crammed into the ballpark to see which team would advance to the World Series. The Red Sox got on the board first with a two-run homer from David Ortiz. They added four more runs in the top of the second with a grand-slam home run from Damon. The Yankees crossed the plate once in the bottom of the third, but Boston promptly answered by sending two runners across in the top of the fourth.

Behind strong pitching from their starter Derek Lowe, the Red Sox maintained their 8–1 lead until the bottom of the seventh. Then Pedro Martinez came in for Lowe—and immediately gave up two doubles and a single to give the Yankees three runs.

Representatives from Red Sox Nation suddenly

turned quiet. Were the Yankees about to mount a game-winning rally?

The answer was no. Martinez settled down and got the next two batters out to end the inning. That was it for him for the game, however. Even though the Sox had sweetened their lead by one with a home run from Mark Bellhorn, they weren't taking any chances. Reliever Mike Timlin came in and sent Derek Jeter, Alex Rodriguez, and Gary Sheffield packing. A sacrifice fly by Boston's Orlando Cabrera gave the Sox an even ten points on the board at the top of the ninth before Yankees pitcher Tom Gordon retired the side.

The Yankees now came to the plate for their last at-bats. They needed seven runs to tie, eight to win. Hideki Matsui started them off with a single. He raced to second when Bernie Williams hit a grounder, but didn't beat the throw. Matsui was out, but Williams was safe at first.

Next up was Jorge Posada. He popped a fly ball to Cabrera at short.

The Red Sox were now just one out away from their first trip to the World Series since 1986. Kenny Lofton came up to bat. He reached first on a walk. Boston changed pitchers again, still not willing to take a risk.

At exactly midnight, pinch hitter Ruben Sierra stepped into the box and faced pitcher Alan Embree. Sierra let the first pitch go by for a ball. He liked the next one and swung. *Crack!* He connected, but not with enough power. The ball bounced toward second. Pokey Reese fielded it cleanly and relayed it to first. Doug Mientkiewicz made the catch and stepped on the bag.

And with that, the stadium erupted with cheers from the Red Sox faithful. The team poured onto the field, laughing and celebrating, and television viewers everywhere leaped and shouted with joy. The Boston club hadn't just won the game, it had made history as the only Major League Baseball team ever to erase a 3–0 game deficit to win a post-season series. It was, as Red Sox owner John Henry declared, "the greatest comeback in baseball history."

"We beat the Yankees," a jubilant Kevin Millar said. "Now they get a chance to watch us on the tube."

Johnny Damon revealed their simple winning

formula: "We stuck together and erased history."

The Red Sox made history again just a week later when, for the first time in eighty-six years, they won the World Series. The Curse of the Bambino had finally been erased, and so long as the team stuck together in the coming seasons as it had during the ALCS, fans believed the curse would never return.

But the team didn't stick together. In fact, by 2006 Johnny Damon, Mark Bellhorn, and Alan Embree had moved to another team. To the great disappointment of Red Sox Nation and the glee of New York fans, their new team was the Yankees.

These players weren't the first to swap red stockings for pinstripes, nor will they be the last. That list is as long and storied as the history of the rivalry itself and includes Major League greats Lou Criger, Patsy Dougherty, Ernie Shore, Carl Mays, Waite Hoyt, Luis Tiant, Wade Boggs, Roger Clemens, Jose Canseco, and, of course, the greatest of them all, Babe Ruth—all were once Red Sox who later became Yankees. (There were plenty of players who went from New York to Boston, too, though if one examines the records, it appears Bos-

27

ton got the short end of the trade stick in most cases!)

Boston and New York haven't met in the post-season since 2004, but the rivalry, now in its second century, is as strong as ever. While the excitement comes from the competitive play on the field, the feud has bubbled up in odd ways off the field as well. Take for example the time a Boston fan tried to curse the Yankees by burying a David Ortiz jersey in the foundation of the new Yankee Stadium. (The shirt was discovered and sold, with the profits going to charity.) Or the Yankees' out-of-this-world decision to award the 2008 season's first pitch to a man about as far from their new stadium as a person could be—astronaut Garrett Reisman, who was on board the International Space Station.

"There are many nations and there is only one universe, and it's a Yankee universe," the lifelong New York fan proclaimed from outer space.

The Yankees do indeed own the baseball universe—on paper, at least. No other Major League team has anywhere near as many World Series rings or had as many marquee players on its roster. But that power has come with a price, earning New York the nickname Evil Empire for its seemingly endless wealth and ruthlessness in going after the best players. By comparison, the Red Sox are the underdog, the sympathy-garnering runner-up in a rivalry that, if history is any guide and the fans have any say, will endure as long as the sport itself exists.

⋆ BY THE NUMBERS ⋆

New York Yankees versus Boston Red Sox
Regular Season History from 1901 to 2010

Total games played	2,082
New York victories*	1,126
Boston victories**	942
Ties (1901–1958)	14

*includes stats as Baltimore Orioles and New York Highlanders
**includes stats as Boston Americans

⋆ WORLD SERIES VICTORIES ⋆

New York 27   **Boston** 7

1923, 1927, 1928, 1932,   1903, 1912, 1915, 1916,
1936, 1937, 1938, 1939,   1918, 2004, 2007
1941, 1943, 1947, 1949,
1950, 1951, 1952, 1953,
1956, 1958, 1961, 1962,
1977, 1978, 1996, 1998,
1999, 2000, 2009

★ CHAPTER TWO ★

The Boston Celtics versus the Los Angeles Lakers

On the night of June 17, 2010, the two greatest basketball dynasties the sport has ever known met on the court for the ultimate showdown: Game Seven of the NBA Finals. The contenders were the mighty Boston Celtics, owners of seventeen championships, the most of any team in the league. Facing them were the equally talented Los Angeles Lakers, who had fifteen rings of their own.

The Celtics and Lakers had battled for the championship eleven times before that night. Boston claimed victory in nine of those matches, the Lakers in two. That lopsided win-loss tally doesn't tell the whole story of the decades-long rivalry between the two clubs. At that story's heart are outstanding player matchups, buzzer-beating shots, overtime duels, and thrilling seventh-game skirmishes.

The Lakers were the first superstars of the National Basketball Association. As a Minneapolis franchise, they posted back-to-back championships in 1949 (when they were part of the Basketball Association of America, or BAA) and 1950, followed by the league's first "three-peat" in 1952, 1953, and 1954. The Celtics were also strong during those years. They reached the playoffs six times from 1951 to 1956 and won their first championship in 1957. As the league's powerhouses, the two teams viewed each other as rivals long before they went head-to-head for the title.

Long anticipated, that matchup finally came in 1959. Spearheading the Lakers' assault were Elgin Baylor and Vern Mikkelsen. Mikkelsen was no stranger to the Finals, having played a vital role in each of the Lakers' five winning title efforts. Now in his last year as a player, he wanted to go out on top.

Rookie Baylor was on the other end of the career spectrum but had already proved his worth. He was the team's high scorer and top rebounder that season, with an average of 24.9 points and fifteen rebounds per game. How much did his contributions matter? Before Baylor joined the roster, the team finished at the bottom with a record of 19–53. After Baylor, the Lakers went 33–39 and reached the Finals.

Anchoring Boston's success was Bill Russell, the center who revolutionized the sport by introducing defense, particularly the blocked shot, as a winning strategy. Besides his incredible athleticism, Russell strengthened the team with his determination and steely nerves. He demonstrated those traits off the court as well as on it, for his transition into a team leader had been anything but smooth.

When Russell joined the Celtics in 1956, there was a huge uproar from many Boston fans because Russell was black. Boston at the time was very prejudiced, and those fans were very vocal. Someone without Russell's mental toughness might have thrown in the towel in the face of such hatred. But Russell stood strong, and when the fans discovered how valuable he was to the team as a rebounder and shot-blocker, they quieted their outcry.

Also playing for the Celtics was the "Houdini

of the Hardwood," Bob Cousy. Cousy had been dazzling fans and opponents since his days playing college basketball at Holy Cross in Worcester, Massachusetts. In 1959, he led the league in assists for the seventh straight year. But he never set himself up to be a star. Rather, he, Russell, and their teammates—Bill Sharman, Frank Ramsey, Sam Jones, and Tom Heinsohn, among others—believed that the only way a team could win was if they played together as a team.

"To me, one of the most beautiful things to see is a group of men coordinating their efforts toward a common goal...to achieve real teamwork in action," Russell once wrote. "I tried to do that, we all tried to do that, on the Celtics. I think we succeeded."

They certainly succeeded in the 1959 Finals. With Russell, Cousy, and the rest of the team playing like a well-oiled machine, they sent the Lakers packing after four games. It was the first sweep in NBA history.

With this same outstanding roster (give or take a couple of players), the Celtics took the title the next two seasons, duplicating the Lakers' three-peat with one of their own. They reached the Finals again in 1962, their sights set on becoming the first team in NBA history to win four rings in a row.

But to achieve that goal, they would have to beat the Lakers, who had also made it to the championship series again—and who, naturally, hoped to unseat the three-time victors and claim the top prize for themselves!

The Lakers, now a Los Angeles franchise, stood a very good chance of doing just that, for their lineup was peppered with talent that year. Elgin Baylor, then the holder of the league's highest single-game point tally with seventy-one, was a constant scoring threat. He was joined by another offensive dynamo, shooting guard Jerry West, to make up the deadly combination of "Mr. Inside" (West) and "Mr. Outside" (Baylor). Rounding out the starting roster were Frank Selvy, Rudy LaRusso, and Ray Felix.

Driven by such talents, the two teams split the first two games, with Boston winning the first 122–108 and Los Angeles the second 129–122. Then came Game Three—and one of the greatest buzzer-beating shots of NBA Finals history.

Played in Los Angeles on April 10 before a

crowd of more than fifteen thousand Lakers fans, Boston had a slim 115–111 lead in the final minute. The game looked in the bag for the Celtics until West got his hands on the ball and sank not one but two jumpers to tie it at 115 each.

With the crowd going crazy, Celtic Sam Jones prepared to inbound the ball from the mid-court sideline. Bob Cousy cut across, his hand reaching for the pass. Jones fired the ball—only to have it picked off by West! With just three seconds left in the game, Cousy dogging his every step, and fans and teammates screaming at him to shoot the jumper, West calmly raced down the length of the court and gently laid the ball in just as the buzzer sounded. The Lakers won 117–115!

"I've never forgotten it," West once recalled of that amazing shot. "Everyone wants to hit a home run in the ninth inning to win a big game. That was my home run."

Unfortunately for Lakers fans, there was no "home run" in the next match, which went to the Celtics 115–103.

Game Five was played back in Boston. There, Elgin Baylor put on a scoring show that left the home team gasping. He hit from inside, outside, baseline, racking up sixty-one of the Lakers' 126 points. His total was the most any player had ever made in a single Finals game, a record that stood until Michael Jordan made sixty-three in 1986. Even better, Los Angeles won 126–121.

The Lakers now needed just one win to beat the Celtics. They didn't get it in Game Six, a 119–105 Boston victory. With the series tied at three each, the teams traveled back to the Boston Garden for the deciding match.

Many sports followers cite Game Seven of the 1962 Finals among the greatest the NBA championship has ever seen. The home team was up 53–47 at the half; near the end of the third quarter, it was still up.

Then Jerry West, known as "Mr. Clutch," took over. As the third quarter wound down, he scored seven straight points to tie it up 75–75.

Things got even more interesting after that. Boston surged ahead. Los Angeles caught up. Boston took the lead again—and again lost it until, with just five seconds left, the score was tied at a hundred points each.

The Lakers had the ball. There was just enough time remaining for one final shot. Baylor, who had thirty-eight points so far, was the obvious go-to man, with West the second choice. But when the moment came, neither was open. So the ball went to Frank Selvy at the baseline.

Selvy was in a groove. Moments before, he had made a driving layup to close the gap to 100–98. He had scored the tying shot as well, after ripping down his own rebound. Now, with the ball in his hands at the baseline, he launched an eight-foot jumper. It was a shot he had made hundreds of times before. But this time, he missed. Bill Russell pulled down the rebound, and the game went into overtime!

"I would trade all my points for that last basket," Selvy later said.

The Celtics added ten more to their side in the extra minutes; the Lakers added only seven. As the last seconds ticked away, Cousy dribbled the ball around the backcourt, evading desperate Los Angeles players until he heard the buzzer sound. Final score: Boston 110, Los Angeles 107. The Celtics were champions again, their fourth title in four years.

Cousy left an enduring image with his overtime dribble, but it was Russell who engineered the win. He was flat-out unstoppable in Game Seven. Not usually an offensive threat, he slipped in thirty points. He also pulled down an astonishing forty rebounds, nineteen of which came in a single quarter, still an NBA record for most rebounds in one quarter. If blocked shots had been a statistic back then, no doubt he would have led in that category as well.

Russell continued to be the driving force for the Celtics in the years that followed. With him leading the charge, Boston won five out of the next six championships. Four of those wins came at the Lakers' expense, for as good as West, Baylor, and the rest of the Lakers were, they just couldn't seem to find an answer for Boston's big man, Bill Russell.

Yet there was one player in the league who regularly gave the Celtic center trouble: Wilt Chamberlain.

Chamberlain was perhaps the most gifted offensive player of all time. In 1959–1960, his rookie season with the Philadelphia Warriors, he scored 2,707 points, earning him the NBA Most Valuable Player and Rookie of the Year awards. Two years later, he made history by shooting a hundred points in a single game.

So what was it like when Chamberlain, the best offensive player, confronted Russell, the best defensive player, on the court?

"Let's see," Russell said after he'd played Chamberlain for the first time. "He's four or five inches taller. He's forty or fifty pounds heavier. His vertical leap is at least as good as mine. He can get up and down the floor as well as I can. And he's smart. The real problem with all this is that I have to show up!"

As sometimes happens when two titanic talents compete, they brought out the best in each other, each challenging the other to show up with his A game every time they played. In one historic match, for example, Chamberlain hit for sixty-two points over Russell—yet Russell's team won, 145–136. Their duels are legendary, the greatest individual NBA rivalry of all time.

In 1968, that rivalry took on new meaning. That's when the Los Angeles Lakers acquired Chamberlain from the Philadelphia 76ers as their solution to Bill Russell. The franchise hoped that

Chamberlain would blend smoothly with Baylor and West—but unfortunately, it didn't work out that way. Chamberlain was used to being a one-man show. His style of play often clashed with that of the others and with the Lakers' coach, Butch van Breda Kolff, as well. Luckily for Lakers fans, Los Angeles found its rhythm, ending in first place with a record of 55–27. The team romped through the postseason by defeating Chamberlain's former team, the Warriors, and the Atlanta Hawks to reach the Finals for the sixth time since moving to Los Angeles.

Once more, their opponents were the Boston Celtics. The Lakers were 0–6 against their number-one rivals in the Finals. But this year, they were feeling very good about their chances, and with good reason, for the fourth-ranked Celtics had limped through the postseason to just barely reach the championships. Plus, this year the Lakers had Wilt Chamberlain.

Chamberlain and Russell had played against each other in seven previous postseason series. Boston came out ahead in six, including the 1964 Finals. Their single loss, to Chamberlain's Philadelphia 76ers in the 1967 Eastern Division

Finals, marked the only break in the Celtics' decade-long playoff domination.

With this kind of history, the two were clearly gunning for each other when their teams faced off for the 1969 NBA Finals. Los Angeles took an early lead in the series, going up 2–0.

Jerry West made the difference in the first game, shooting fifty-three of the Lakers' 120 points when Russell, now the Celtics' coach as well as starting center, decided not to double-team him. As amazing as West was, it was Chamberlain who had the play of the game, scoring the winning basket with just twenty-three seconds left on the clock.

After West's offensive onslaught in Game One, Russell slapped an extra defender on West to slow him down. But it didn't stop West—and once more he took full advantage. He ended with forty-one points in the Lakers' 118–112 win.

Russell had learned his lesson. Down 0–2, he instructed his players to shut down West in their third meeting. The strategy helped; the Celtics won 111–105. They won the next outing, too, although it wasn't a pretty game for either squad, with a combined total of fifty turnovers.

The hero of the night was Sam Jones. With seven seconds remaining, he used a triple-pick set by teammates John Havlicek, Bailey Howell, and Larry Siegfried to boost a shot over Chamberlain's outstretched fingers. Even though he slipped while releasing the ball, Jones's shot went in, giving Boston the 89–88 win.

The fifth game was a Lakers victory, but it came with a hefty price tag. Jerry West pulled a hamstring muscle while trying to stop a Celtics drive. He played in Game Six but was limping so badly that he was no longer the scoring threat he'd been. The Celtics won 99–90 to force a Game Seven.

Despite West's condition, many predicted that the Lakers would beat the Celtics in the final match. The Lakers' owner, Jack Kent Cooke, was so confident that Baylor, West, and Chamberlain would earn the title that he ordered thousands of balloons to be suspended in the Los Angeles arena's rafters. When the Lakers beat the Celtics on their home court, those balloons would drop down to kick off a huge celebration.

West was furious when he learned about the balloons. He guessed that Bill Russell would use

Cooke's arrogant gesture to motivate his team. He was right.

"They can't beat us," Russell told his teammates in the locker room before the game. "But it's going to be funny watching them take down those balloons."

Just as West had feared, Russell's speech fired up the Celtics. They captured and held the lead for most of the game. But the Lakers weren't beaten. They drew inspiration from West, who was still potent despite his injury. Chamberlain was also in pain from an injured knee early in the fourth period. Late in the fourth period, he watched the game from the sidelines.

Fortunately for Lakers fans, West and Chamberlain's replacement, Mel Counts, fired in key baskets late in the game. With just three minutes remaining, the score was Boston 103, Los Angeles 102.

That's where the score stayed as the clock ticked down. Then suddenly—*whap!*—West knocked the ball away from Boston's Havlicek. But the steal attempt backfired, for the ball flew right into Celtic Don Nelson's hands. Nelson lofted a shot. The ball hit the rim, caromed straight up into the air, and then—*swish!*—fell right through the net! Boston was up 105–102.

The Lakers tried to take over but couldn't. Siegfried hit two free throws to give the Celtics a five-point lead with just twenty-two seconds remaining. One more from the line made it Boston 108–102—and fans started streaming out of the arena. Los Angeles added four more points in the final seconds, but it was too late. The Celtics took the win with a final score of 108–106—and Cooke's balloons stayed right where they were.

All the Lakers were upset, but Jerry West was downright bereft. He had played his heart out that night, earning a triple-double with forty-two points, thirteen rebounds, and twelve assists. For that performance and his others in the series, he was named the Finals MVP—the only player from a losing team ever to win that award.

Nothing could have pleased Bill Russell more, for he greatly admired West. "Los Angeles has not won the championship," he commented, "but Jerry West is a champion."

Russell was a champion as well. He retired after

that seventh game with eleven rings, the most of any player in the history of the NBA. He was truly one of the greatest players of his era, but as his teammate Don Nelson once said, "There are two types of superstars. One makes himself look good at the expense of the other guys on the floor. But there's another type who makes the players around him look better than they are, and that's the type Russell was."

And as for the rivalry between Wilt Chamberlain and Bill Russell, perhaps their total matchup tallies speak for themselves. Of the 142 games they played from 1959 to 1969, Russell's Celtics won eighty-five while Chamberlain's teams—the Warriors, the 76ers, and the Lakers—took just fifty-seven.

In the years that followed the Celtics' eleventh title, Los Angeles and Boston added three more rings each to their collections. But it wasn't until 1984 that the two met in the Finals again. Fans were in a frenzy of excitement at the renewal of their favorite East versus West, Beantown grit versus Hollywood glitz rivalry. They were also delighted to watch a classic player matchup: Bird versus Magic.

Celtic Larry Bird and Laker Earvin "Magic" Johnson already had a ferocious on-court feud going when they entered the NBA in 1979. Earlier that same year, Johnson's college team, Michigan State University, had beaten Bird's undefeated Indiana State University in the NCAA championship game. That televised match was watched by more people than any other college game at the time, making Bird and Magic household heroes overnight.

Players of their caliber were exactly what the NBA needed just then, for the league was in the midst of a financial slump. Bird's and Magic's dynamic styles captivated audiences and rejuvenated the NBA's flagging ratings. "We came along at the right time," Magic agreed. "We pushed each other, meant so much to each other, and meant so much to the game."

Seeing the two players together on the court was a rarity, however, because their teams met just twice during the regular season. So when the Lakers and the Celtics reached the Finals in 1984, basketball lovers everywhere rejoiced.

It had all the makings of a fantastic series. Both

teams had ended in first place in their divisions, although the Celtics had the better record, 62–20 to the Lakers' 54–28. Two of Los Angeles's regular-season wins had been over Boston, however, which gave them an edge. Both teams had rosters positively loaded with talent including Kareem Abdul-Jabbar and James Worthy for the Lakers, and Kevin McHale and Robert Parish for the Celtics. And of course, there were Bird and Magic, veterans with five years' experience each and plenty of gas left in their tanks to fuel them for years to come.

The first game was played in the Boston Garden. The Lakers went right to work, using their trademark "run-'n'-gun" offensive to go up 24–9 after seven minutes. Magic was masterly, driving down the court on breakaways and muscling in for crucial rebounds. He also dished the assists to Abdul-Jabbar, helping him to thirty-two points. The Celtics did their best, but that night their best wasn't good enough. The Lakers won 115–109.

Game Two was an edge-of-the-seat nail-biter that very likely would have ended in another Lakers victory if not for Celtic Gerald Henderson.

With just eighteen seconds on the clock and the score Los Angeles 113, Boston 111, James Worthy lofted a pass toward Byron Scott from under the Celtics' hoop. Suddenly, Henderson swept in, stole the ball, and rolled into the basket to tie the score at 113 each. The Celtics went on to win 124–121 in overtime.

"I could see the seams of the ball, like it was spinning in slow motion," Lakers head coach Pat Riley recalled of Worthy's stolen pass, "but I couldn't do anything about it."

Unfortunately for Boston fans, there would be no such last-second heroics in Game Three. In fact, there was nothing heroic about the Celtics at all that night. The Lakers demolished their rivals 137–104. Magic was particularly devastating, delivering twenty-one assists.

Bird, who had drained thirty points, was livid at the loss. "We played like a bunch of sissies," he railed at his teammates.

In response, the Celtics came out swinging in Game Four—literally. In one particularly aggressive play, Kevin McHale clotheslined Laker Kurt Rambis to stop him from scoring. The foul wasn't sportsmanlike—not by a long shot—but it did seem to make the Lakers stop and think.

"Before Kevin McHale hit Kurt Rambis, the Lakers were just running across the street whenever they wanted," Celtic Cedric Maxwell said of that moment. "Now they stop at the corner, push the button, wait for the light, and look both ways."

Bird, meanwhile, had the shot of the game. With seventeen seconds left in overtime and the score tied at 123, he wrestled free of Magic, nabbed a pass, and stuck a fadeaway jumper. The Celtics went on to win 129–125.

Game Five, nicknamed the "Heat Game" because of the extreme temperature in the Boston Garden, went to the home team 121–103. But Los Angeles evened the series in Game Six 119–108. For the fourth time in their shared Finals history, the championship would be decided by Game Seven.

The contest was played in Boston. Chants of "Beat LA!" reverberated throughout the Garden for the entire match, spurring the Celtics on to a commanding fourteen-point lead late in the game. But the Lakers surged back until, with just over a minute remaining in the game, they had cut the lead to three. They couldn't seal the deal, however. A last-minute steal by Maxwell followed by a pair of free throws from Dennis Johnson ended the game—and the eighth Celtics-Lakers championship—in Boston's favor yet again. Final score: Boston 111, Lakers 102.

Lakers fans couldn't believe it. Was their team doomed to lose to the Celtics every time?

That question was answered a year later in the much-hyped and greatly anticipated rematch between Bird's Celtics and Magic's Lakers. Both teams were at the top of their games; Boston finished with their best record in years, 63–19, one win more than the Lakers' 62–20. They had split their two regular-season games, leaving fans wondering which of the equally dominating teams would come out on top this year.

If the first match was any indication, the Celtics were going to win. They absolutely destroyed the Lakers, serving them a loss so lopsided that it became known as the "Memorial Day Massacre." Abdul-Jabbar, usually a threat under the hoop, was held to twelve points and three rebounds in the

148–114 defeat. The Celtics, by comparison, couldn't seem to miss if they tried. "It was one of those days," Celtics coach K.C. Jones said, "where if you turn around and close your eyes, the ball's gonna go in."

The Lakers were down but far from out. Abdul-Jabbar returned to form for Game Two, posting thirty points, seventeen rebounds, eight assists, and three blocked shots to help Los Angeles to a 109–102 victory. The series moved to California for Game Three, and there the Lakers had their fun with the Celtics, winning 136–111. Abdul-Jabbar made history that night, surpassing Wilt Chamberlain as the league's all-time playoff scorer.

Boston squeaked in a win the next match, 107–105, to stay alive, but dropped Game Five to go down 3–2 in the series.

Game Six was played in front of thousands of screaming Boston fans in the Garden. Those screams turned into groans of disbelief when, after eight defeats at the hands of the Celtics in eight Finals, the Lakers finally beat their archrivals. The hero of the night was again Abdul-Jabbar. The lanky Laker center chased loose balls, ripped down rebounds, drove the length of the court, and stuck his signature shot, the skyhook.

"What you saw was passion," Coach Riley later said of his star center.

Magic helped reverse the curse, too, by contributing a triple-double effort to the victory. Final score: Lakers 111, Celtics 100.

To no one's surprise, Abdul-Jabbar was awarded the Finals MVP trophy. But it was the gleaming O'Brien NBA championiship trophy that took center stage that night. As the Lakers' owner, Jerry Buss, famously said, "This trophy removes the most odious sentence in the English language. It can never be said again that the Lakers have never beaten the Celtics."

Los Angeles proved that the win was no fluke by defeating the Celtics in the Finals again in 1987. That loss marked the beginning of the end for Boston's decades-long reign. It would be more than twenty years before the Celtics returned to the Finals. The Lakers won their eleventh overall title in 1988 and surged to greatness again in the early 2000s, three-peating with a roster that included Shaquille O'Neal and Kobe Bryant.

Meanwhile, the Celtics-Lakers rivalry went into a twenty-one-year hibernation. Then, in 2008, it awakened, dusted itself off, and returned to the spotlight. The players had all changed since their last meeting, of course, but the game they played was the same. Laker Kobe Bryant, a one-man scoring machine, was the superstar of Los Angeles's lineup. True to their team's tradition, the Celtics spread the scoring wealth around more, relying on Kevin Garnett, Paul Pierce, and Ray Allen to rack up the points.

Rack up the points is just what they did in three out of the first five games of the series. In Game Six, they manufactured the most devastating offensive rout in the Celtics-Lakers history, a 131–92 blowout that saw Garnett and Allen tallying twenty-six points and Pierce seventeen.

When the final buzzer sounded, the Celtics had championship number seventeen, the most of any team in the NBA. As the players and fans celebrated, Kevin Garnett searched the stands for a man who knew exactly what he was feeling at that moment: Bill Russell. When he found him, the two shared a hug and wide smiles.

"I hope we made you proud," Garnett said to the living legend.

"You sure did," Russell replied.

The Celtics had now beaten the Lakers in nine out of eleven meetings. When they faced Los Angeles in the Finals again in 2010, they hoped to make it an even ten. The Lakers, defending champs with another title in 2009, were just as eager for the win. Both teams battled ferociously, knotting the series at three games each.

Then came the ultimate showdown, the June 17 match that decided the world champion of 2010. It was the fifth time in the franchises' shared history that they'd reached a seventh game. If history had repeated itself, the Celtics would have won that seventh game as they had the four previous times.

But this go-around, the Lakers were not to be denied. They erased a thirteen-point deficit in the second quarter only to fall behind again before the halftime break. Still behind by two going into the final quarter, they came alive to capture the lead. The Celtics fought back to draw within two points with just sixteen seconds remaining.

That's as close as Boston came to capturing their

eighteenth ring. With the score 81–79, the Lakers hit two free throws. Final score: Lakers 83, Celtics 79.

How did Kobe Bryant, the Finals MVP, feel about beating his team's number-one rival? Before the series began, he would have said he wasn't even thinking about that. But afterward, the truth came out.

"I was just lying to you guys," he confessed to the media. "I know every Celtics series. I know every statistic. [Winning this Finals] meant the world to me."

As well it should, for there is no greater prize in professional basketball than the NBA championship. And when the two most storied dynasties in the sport's history go head-to-head to win that prize, there is no greater basketball action to be seen. No doubt there will be more Celtics-Lakers confrontations to come—and nothing would make the players or their fans happier.

⋆ BY THE NUMBERS ⋆

Boston Celtics versus Los Angeles Lakers
Regular Season History from
1948–1949 to 2009–2010

Total games played	272
Boston victories	152
Los Angeles victories	120

⋆ NBA CHAMPIONSHIPS ⋆

Boston 17	**Los Angeles** 16
1957, 1959, 1960, 1961, 1962, 1963, 1964, 1965, 1966, 1968, 1969, 1974, 1976, 1981, 1984, 1986, 2008	1949,* 1950,* 1952,* 1953,* 1954,* 1972, 1980, 1982, 1985, 1987, 1988, 2000, 2001, 2002, 2009, 2010

*Won when franchise was in Minneapolis

★ CHAPTER THREE ★

D.C. United versus
the Los Angeles Galaxy

The field at Foxboro Stadium in Massachusetts was a sea of mud-slick grass on October 20, 1996. It had been raining hard all day. The temperature hovered around forty-five degrees. Fans in the stands huddled together under umbrellas, raincoats, and anything else they could find to keep the rain off. Many of them were already soaked, but they didn't care. They were about to witness a new chapter in U.S. soccer history unfold.

On the field, the players ignored the weather. Instead, they focused their attention on a short, stocky midfielder named Marco "El Diablo" Etcheverry. Etcheverry was about to take a corner kick. As he readied himself, his D.C. United teammates and Los Angeles Galaxy opponents jockeyed for position in front of the Galaxy's goal.

A second later, spectators witnessed one of the greatest moments in Major League Soccer (MLS). Etcheverry blasted the kick. The ball rocketed over and past several players. Then United's Eddie Pope leaped and headed the ball. It flew into the net, billowing the back strings. Goal!

The Washington, D.C., squad and its fans went crazy. Pope, grinning ear-to-ear, launched himself in a headfirst slide across the wet grass in celebration. He had every reason to rejoice. His goal had come in sudden-death overtime, breaking a 2–2 tie to win the match for the Black-and-Red. And not just any match—this was the 1996 MLS Cup, the first championship game of the brand-new U.S. professional soccer organization.

It was a match that might never have happened if not for another championship, the 1994 World Cup. Outside the United States, soccer is the most popular sport in most countries, and the World Cup is its premier event. In 1993, the United States made a bid to host the prestigious monthlong competition. The Fédération Internationale de Football Association (FIFA), the governing body of soccer, was willing to consider the bid on one condition: The United States had to create a top-tier professional soccer league. The United States readily agreed.

Three years later, in the spring of 1996, Major League Soccer opened its first season.

The league was made up of ten teams divided into the Eastern Conference and the Western Conference. Each team had a roster of twenty-four players. Twenty of those players were selected from a draft. The other four were drawn from a pool of top national and international players who had agreed to play in the MLS.

These marquee players were considered a crucial element to the league's success. First of all, they would bring a high caliber of play to the games, and well-played matches always generate more interest in a sport than ones played poorly. To make sure games would be competitive, players were distributed evenly throughout the clubs to ensure that no one team was stacked with talent.

Second and equally important, many of these star athletes already had huge numbers of fans in the United States. These fans included a large immigrant population, people who up until now had been forced to follow their favorite international players through the media. Thanks to the MLS, these players were coming to the United States—and the league hoped their loyal fans would pack the stadiums to see them in action, for the more fans who came to games, the more likely the start-up league would succeed.

The one drawback to hiring these top players was that many of them were also key elements for their countries' national teams. Those national teams demanded that the players be available for important matches, such as World Cup qualifiers and the Olympics. Such a demand was the norm throughout the soccer world, and since the United States had its own national team that it wanted filled with its own best players, the league's founders agreed to release the athletes when necessary.

The inaugural MLS season had a schedule of thirty-two games, played from April through October. At the end of the season, the best four teams in each conference took part in the playoffs. The winners of the quarterfinals advanced to the semifinal rounds. The winners of those matches, one from the East and one from the West, faced each other for the MLS Cup. In 1996, those teams were the Los Angeles Galaxy and D.C. United.

That couldn't have been better news for the MLS. Both teams had put together exciting seasons. Both drew big crowds, including D.C. United's energetic and very vocal *La Barra Brava* (translation: Brave Fans), whose members sang, danced, and cheered for their favorite United players throughout home games. Both boasted talented players who dazzled spectators with remarkable fleet-footed plays. And their meeting fit the model of a classic sports rivalry, East Coast versus West Coast.

United had given their fans plenty to cheer about in the second half of the season. After a faltering start, the team had surged to finish 16–16.* Credit for the turnaround fell in large part to emerging star Jaime Moreno. A native of Bolivia,

---

*More precisely, with fifteen wins, thirteen losses, one shoot-out win/tie, and three shoot-out losses/ties. MLS rules from 1996 to 1999 had tie games ending with a penalty shoot-out. Each team had five chances for a player to make a goal one-on-one against the goalkeeper. At the end, the team that scored the most goals in the shoot-out was declared the winner. The point system awarded three for a win in regulation time, one for a win in a shoot-out, and none for a loss, regulation or shoot-out.

As of 2000, the MLS bowed to the more traditional, international rule that had tie games go into overtime. If no team had scored after two five-minute periods, then the match was declared a tie. The league also adopted the international point system that awarded three points for a win, one for each team for a tie, and none for a loss.

Moreno had joined the Washington club midway through the schedule. His amazing skill had an immediate effect on the team.

So did his experience playing with Marco Etcheverry. The two had been teammates on the Bolivian national team. Now teammates on United, they worked magic together on the field, with Etcheverry often playing a role in Moreno's goals. D.C.'s success came from more than these two players, of course. Forward Raul Diaz Arce scored the second-most goals in the league. Defenders Jeff Agoos and Eddie Pope added power in the backfield. Versatile Tony Sanneh contributed strength in various positions. When the roster jelled, the team chalked up seven wins in their last eleven games, including a 2–1 victory over the Galaxy on August 18.

Los Angeles had plenty of experienced talent and fan favorites, too. Burly striker Eduardo "El Tanque" Hurtado was the team's top goal-maker. With midfielders Cobi Jones and Mauricio Cienfuegos consistently feeding him the ball, he notched forty-nine points on twenty-one goals and seven assists. The Galaxy also boasted one of the league's best goalkeepers, Jorge Campos, who finished the regular season with the lowest goals-against average of 1.20.

The Los Angeles squad meshed well from the start. The Galaxy racked up eight straight victories, including their season opener, which saw them pack the stands with a record crowd of nearly seventy thousand fans. Although they suffered a midseason slump, they ended with a record of nineteen wins and thirteen losses to finish in first place in the West. They then pushed their way through the playoffs, besting the San Jose Clash (now the Earthquakes) two games to one in the best-of-three series. Next to fall were the Kansas City Wizards, whom they beat in two straight games to reach the MLS Cup finals.

Meanwhile, United dispatched the New Jersey/New York MetroStars (now the Red Bulls) two out of three and then stunned the soccer world by defeating the best team in the league, the Tampa Bay Mutiny, in matches that ended 4–1 and 2–1. Now all that stood in the way of their winning the championship was the Galaxy.

Sometimes, soccer games can go scoreless for

long stretches of time. Not this one. After just five minutes of play, Hurtado made history by blasting the league's first finals goal into the net. Los Angeles had reason to celebrate again later in the game when Chris Armas added a second for their side to make it Galaxy 2, United 0.

That's where the score stayed until the seventy-second minute. D.C. was awarded a free kick, which Etcheverry booted from far outside the goal box. The blast was hard and high, and the ball sizzled toward the Galaxy's goal. D.C.'s Tony Sanneh saw his chance. He leaped and headed the ball right into the net. Goal for United!

Less than ten minutes later, Shawn Medved converted another Etcheverry free kick to even the score at 2–2. Both teams tried to unravel the knot in the final minutes. But when regulation time ended, it was still tied up, sending the match into sudden-death overtime. That's when Eddie Pope made his now-famous game-winning header—and equally famous slide.

Ten days after taking the MLS championship, D.C. United won the oldest and most prestigious soccer competition in the United States, the

Lamar Hunt U.S. Open Cup. This competition saw play among teams from the MLS as well as lower-tiered professional and amateur leagues. With their victory over all challengers, United cemented their place as the number-one team in the country.

It also made them the team all other clubs in the MLS wanted to beat in the coming season. Chief among those targeting the Black-and-Red was the runner-up in the MLS Cup, the Galaxy.

The California team hardly provided much of a threat at first, however, for it posted losses in seven of its first eight matches. Four games later, the club's management made a radical change, replacing its head coach with assistant coach Octavio Zambrano.

The switch proved to be just what the Galaxy needed. They won five of their next seven games, including a decisive 3–1 victory against defending champion D.C. United. Los Angeles continued to play well and in the last month of the season posted a six-game winning streak to rise from the cellar to second place with a record of sixteen wins and sixteen losses. That was as far as the Galaxy went that year, however. The Dallas Burn smoked them two games to one in the semifinals, ending the Galaxy's bid for their first MLS Cup.

United had followed up their first successful season with an even better one, finishing at the top of the ranks with twenty-one wins and eleven losses. They continued to dominate in the postseason, running over the New England Revolution and the Columbus Crew to face the Colorado Rapids in their second consecutive MLS Cup bid. On October 26, before a sellout hometown crowd of more than fifty-seven thousand fans, Moreno and Sanneh each booted in a goal to give their team a 2–1 victory over the Rapids.

With back-to-back MLS Cups, the D.C. team was on a path to becoming the league's first true dynasty. But hot on their heels in 1998 were their cross-country rivals, the Los Angeles Galaxy.

Two near misses at the top MLS prize made the California team more determined than ever to emerge as league champs that year. With that goal in mind, the Galaxy positively flew out of the starting gate, winning seventeen of their first nineteen matches! Those games saw them posting some of the highest scores in the league, including an 8–1 blowout against the team that had sent them packing in the 1997 postseason, the Dallas Burn.

Then they came face-to-face with D.C. United. The Black-and-Red had put together a strong season as well, nine victories and seven ties to start the year. Now, on July 10, they did what no other team had done, namely, shut out the Galaxy with a score of three goals to none. They did it again two weeks later, needing just a single goal to take the win.

Those losses were not the norm for the Los Angeles squad, which went on to finish with twenty-four wins and eight defeats for a league high of sixty-eight points. They also made the record books by posting the greatest number of goals in a single season with eighty-five in thirty-two games, while allowing just forty-four goals to be scored against them. They earned the highest assist total, too, with 104. With those stats behind them, confidence was high that the Galaxy would reach the MLS Cup finals that year.

Confidence was equally high that their rivals for the Cup would be D.C. United, whose season had been nearly as good as the Galaxy's. United finished 24–8, but with fewer overall points than the Galaxy since seven of D.C.'s wins came on shoot-outs. They also won the honor of becoming the first MLS team to win the CONCACAF Champions Cup, an international competition held in midsummer among teams from North America, Central America, and the Caribbean.

As the postseason approached, fans eagerly anticipated a rematch of the 1996 MLS Cup. But it was not to be. While United moved past the Miami Fusion and the Columbus Crew in the playoffs, the Galaxy were snuffed out by the Chicago Fire in the Western Conference finals. The Fire went on to win the 1998 championship, shutting out United 2–0.

D.C. United fans were disappointed in their team's second-best status in the Cup. They were even more disheartened when they learned of big changes to their team for the 1999 season, the biggest of which came just two days after the Fire defeated them. That's when head coach Bruce Arena announced he was leaving to assume duties with the U.S. national team. In addition to Arena, two key players from United switched to different teams. John Harkes went to the New England Revolution, and Tony Sanneh went overseas to Germany.

Fortunately, many of the team's core players remained, including Moreno, Etcheverry, Pope, and Agoos. Also returning were high-scoring forward Roy Lassiter and the 1998 Rookie of the Year, Ben Olsen, a standout midfielder who had tallied four goals and eight assists in his first season with United. Under the guidance of their new coach, Thomas Rongen, D.C. romped to the top of the Eastern Conference with twenty-three wins and nine losses for fifty-seven points.

Meanwhile, after a tight contest among four of the six Western Conference teams—the league had expanded by two teams in 1998—the Galaxy emerged in first place with twenty wins and twelve losses. It was their second season with twenty or more victories, the first of any team in the MLS to achieve that benchmark. Their shining star was goalkeeper Kevin Hartman, who set a league record for goals-against average with an astounding 0.91, or less than one goal per game!

With their loyal fans chanting and cheering for them every step of the way, the Galaxy surpassed the Colorado Rapids and the Dallas Burn to reach the final round of the MLS Cup. It had been three years since they'd last made it so far in the postseason, and this time, they were in it to win it.

"You want to be in first place, you want to be the best team," Galaxy Cobi Jones pointed out. "And to do that, you've got to win this game."

Winning the game meant defeating a familiar foe: D.C. United, who were still burning from their defeat in the championship in 1998. "Frustrated and angry" was how Jeff Agoos described the team's feelings about the loss. "The only success for us would be getting back to the MLS Cup and winning it."

Nearly forty-five thousand fans turned out for the historic rematch in Foxboro Stadium. Unlike the rain-soaked inaugural Cup in 1996, the weather on this November afternoon was warm and sunny. The players took the field amid resounding cheers from the packed stands.

Those cheers grew louder for the Galaxy as Cobi Jones battled with defenders in front of the D.C.

goal, trying desperately but failing to put the ball into the net. Seven minutes into the match, those cheers turned to gasps of alarm. That's when the Galaxy's captain and star defender, Robin Fraser, was shoved from behind by D.C.'s Lassiter while the two were chasing after the ball. Fraser fell, hitting the turf so hard he broke his collarbone. Soccer is a physical sport, and injuries like this do happen, but when no foul was called, the Galaxy and their fans were outraged.

"To lose that player in the first few minutes of the game, it throws everything out of whack," Jones later said.

Los Angeles certainly looked out of whack when, nineteen minutes into the game, a throw-in by Etcheverry was headed into prime scoring position— by a Galaxy player! Lassiter tried to convert the blunder into a goal. Hartman made the save, but he sent the ball bouncing right back to Lassiter. The ricochet landed in front of Moreno, who quickly tapped the ball past the sprawling Hartman and into the net.

Goal!

United fans went wild, spraying confetti into the air and leaping from their seats. They grew very

Bill Russell of the Boston Celtics and Wilt Chamberlain of the Los Angeles Lakers epitomize the rivalry between these two legendary basketball teams. Here, in the 1969 NBA Finals, Russell stuffs the ball through the hoop despite Chamberlain's best efforts to stop him.

AP/Wide World Photos

A most unusual photograph, taken in 1947, of George Stanley Halas (left), coach of the Chicago Bears, and Earl "Curly" Lambeau, coach of the Green Bay Packers. They seem to be sharing a laugh, but in truth, the two men hated each other. Their personal animosity undoubtedly sparked the longtime rivalry between their teams.

Former Red Sox pitcher Babe Ruth shows Boston what it lost when it traded him to the New York Yankees by sliding safely into second base.

Hockey is a contact sport…and when the game is Canadiens versus Bruins, that contact is often fierce, as this body check clearly shows.

Two superstars of Major League Soccer battle it out in a 2009
match: David Beckham (left) of the Los Angeles Galaxy versus Jaime
Moreno of D.C. United.

It's a classic matchup: A Packers fan—in "Cheesehead" gear—and a Bears fan pretend to fight before one of the teams' 2010 games.

The symbol of the sweep is held aloft by Boston Red Sox fans after their team defeated its archrival, the New York Yankees, in a three-game series in 2009.

Lakers fans "wig out" before Game Five of the 2010 NBA Finals against the Boston Celtics.

quiet soon afterward, however, for their defense almost made an own goal. But instead of going past D.C.'s goalie into the net, the ball rocketed skyward and bounced harmlessly away.

Not long afterward, the Galaxy nearly suffered another enormous setback. During a United attack on the Galaxy's goal, Moreno collided with Hartman, knocking him hard on the head. Hartman lay on the ground for several long seconds, clutching his skull in obvious pain. He stayed in the game, although he may have wished he hadn't.

A few minutes after being hit, Hartman flubbed a kick on a routine clear. He recovered the ball just outside the penalty box but then made another error. Instead of booting the ball far upfield, he tried to pass it to a teammate near the sideline—but dug his foot through the ground instead of connecting solidly with the ball!

The ball wound up in front of D.C.'s Ben Olsen. With Hartman still outside the box, Olsen needed just one massive kick to make it United 2, Galaxy 0.

"It just popped right to me. It was heaven-sent," Olsen said.

There was still half a game to be played after Olsen's goal, but try as they might, the Galaxy couldn't get on the board. D.C. didn't score again either, but it didn't have to. When the last seconds had ticked off the clock, the fans erupted with roars of approval. D.C. United were the MLS Cup champs for the third time!

"What we have done in four years is incredible, absolutely incredible," a tired but overjoyed Jeff Agoos marveled.

In the Galaxy locker room, Hartman slumped on a bench, heartbroken. "I feel like I stole money from my teammates and stole money from the fans," he murmured, settling the blame for the loss fully on his shoulders.

Hartman more than made up for his mistakes in the first game against D.C. in 2000. He rejected all shots on goal to blank United while his teammates slammed four shots into the net behind his counterpart, Tom Presthus.

"The players are very embarrassed," United's coach, Thomas Rongen, said after the upset. The Galaxy "got some measure of revenge today."

That may have been true, but it wasn't enough

for the Los Angeles team. "Revenge will only come when we raise the MLS Cup," their coach stated.

Unfortunately for Galaxy fans, their team failed to achieve that goal in 2000. While Los Angeles came in second in the West to reach the playoffs for the fifth time in five years, they fell to the eventual champions, the Kansas City Wizards, in the semifinals.

As disappointed as the Galaxy's faithful fans were, it was nothing compared with how D.C.'s fans felt at the season's end. After four years of league domination, the Washington squad dropped straight down into the cellar. They won just eight of thirty-two games played!

The Galaxy and United might have had stronger seasons if not for their ever-changing rosters. That year was the start of World Cup qualifiers as well as the 2000 Olympics in Sydney, Australia. Several key players from D.C. and Los Angeles played for the U.S. national team and were absent during the season because of overseas commitments. Without a consistent lineup, it was nearly impossible for either squad to find its rhythm—although clearly, the Galaxy were much more successful than their cross-country rivals.

In the years that followed, many would question whether there actually was a rivalry between the two anymore. Rivalries are fiercest when both teams have similar records. But in 2001 and 2002, D.C. United continued to wallow at the bottom of the rankings while the Los Angeles Galaxy surged to the top. In 2002, the Galaxy thrilled their fans by defeating the New England Revolution to take their first MLS Cup. It looked as though the rivalry might resurface in 2003, when both clubs ended in fourth place in their conferences, but hope of a historic third D.C.–Los Angeles MLS Cup died when neither team made it past the semifinals. United reclaimed their championship status with a victory in the 2004 Cup, but the win was over the Kansas City Wizards, not the Galaxy, who were out of the postseason in the conference finals.

Determined to come back stronger than ever in 2005, the Galaxy boosted their roster and their fan base with the addition of superstar Landon Donovan. They boosted their rankings as well to reach the final round of the postseason. Unfortunately for fans of the rivalry, their foes weren't the defending champs, for D.C. had bowed out in the quarterfinals. Instead, the Galaxy faced—and beat—the Revolution.

The Los Angeles–D.C. feud retreated even further from the minds of soccer fans in 2006, when United fell in the Eastern Conference semifinals and the Galaxy failed to make the playoffs for the first time in their history. Then came 2007—and one of the most significant developments ever in Major League Soccer.

The MLS had evolved greatly since 1996. Teams had been added and disbanded. The league had split into three conferences and then regrouped back into two. Rules had been adjusted to conform to international standards. Soccer-specific stadiums had been constructed to draw in fans. Hotshot players such as D.C. United's fourteen-year-old phenom Freddy Adu had grabbed national sports headlines. All the changes were good for the league and its image. But they paled in comparison to the day in 2007 when David Beckham, one of the most popular soccer players in the world, announced he had signed with the Los Angeles Galaxy.

The media frenzy that surrounded Beckham's

move to the MLS was enormous. People the world over couldn't wait to see how he would perform on his new team. For Beckham's part, he was hoping to do for the MLS what the greatest soccer player ever, Pelé, had done for the defunct National American Soccer League in the 1970s and 1980s—namely, make the sport more popular in the United States.

Fans were kept waiting longer than expected for Beckham's highly publicized entrance into the MLS, for ankle and knee problems delayed his debut. Finally, on August 9, 2007, the celebrity midfielder took to the field for his first MLS game. His team's opponent? D.C. United.

The field in Washington's RFK Stadium was rain-soaked that day, as were the more than forty-six thousand fans in the stands. Still troubled by his injuries, Beckham didn't start the game. But seventy-one minutes into the match, he got up from the bench, switched into his team jersey amid great applause, and trotted out onto the field. The crowd roared with happiness. At last, the man they had come to see was about to play!

D.C. was in the lead then, having scored the

game's only goal in the twenty-seventh minute. The Galaxy were playing shorthanded because of the red-card ejection of Kyle Martino three minutes earlier. Beckham almost helped Los Angeles even the score at the eighty-four-minute mark with his first MLS free kick. The kick was true, but his teammate Carlos Pavon deflected it too high. The game ended soon afterward with the score still D.C. 1, Los Angeles 0.

It was a different story when the clubs met again less than a week later. For one thing, they weren't playing in a regular-season MLS game. Rather, the match was part of a new Mexico-U.S. competition called SuperLiga. The tournament started on July 24, and games were held in different venues around the country. The early stages found four teams from the MLS competing against one another and against four teams from Mexico. By the semifinals, three teams from the U.S.—the Houston Dynamo, D.C. United, and the Los Angeles Galaxy—and one from Mexico, the Pachuca, remained. The Pachuca eliminated the Dynamo, leaving the Galaxy and United to battle for the open spot in the finals.

The game was held on August 15 on the Galaxy's home field, the Home Depot Center in Carson, California. "Tonight, the two most decorated sides in Major League Soccer history are on display," the television announcer declared before the match.

Also on display were the talents of David Beckham, who started the game. He brought the fans to their feet just by being on the field, but it was what he did in the twenty-seventh minute that had them jumping with joy. Los Angeles had been awarded a free kick twenty-seven yards outside D.C.'s goal. Beckham was the master in these situations, noted for "bending" the ball with such skill that goalkeepers had trouble stopping his kicks. But could he do it now?

He could! With D.C. players lining up in front of the goal mouth, Beckham booted a strong blast over United's wall, past D.C. goalie Troy Perkins, and into the net.

Beckham had a hand—or rather, a foot—in the Galaxy's second goal, too. The play came just minutes into the second half. Beckham had the ball near midfield. Landon Donovan was running free farther down. Beckham threaded a pass to him. Donovan raced with the ball toward the D.C. goal. Perkins came out to challenge. Donovan stutter-stepped and then walloped the ball past him to make it 2–0. D.C. tried to catch up but couldn't. The Galaxy took the win and went on to face Pachuca, who beat them 4–3 in the final round of SuperLiga.

Despite this strong showing and the attention on the club thanks to Beckham, all was not well with the Galaxy. They finished the season in fifth place to miss the playoffs for the second year in a row. The disappointments continued for D.C. United, too. After ending with the best record in the league, they were defeated in the semifinals of the MLS Cup.

The next year was another low point in the Galaxy's history. After a strong start, the club faltered, at one point going twelve games without a win. In August, the management made a change. Head coach Ruud Gullit was out. In his place was Bruce Arena, the onetime D.C. coach. While the team still struggled despite the talents of Beckham, Donovan, and their second-highest scorer,

Edson Buddle, and ended 2008 with a record of 8–13–9, they had confidence that Arena would soon help them turn around.

They were right. In 2009 the Arena-led Galaxy rocketed back to the top of the Western Conference and a year later were in first place in the league with a record of 18–7–5. D.C. United, meanwhile, finished tied for eighth overall in 2009, and in 2010, they ended in the cellar with just six wins.

With one team high up the ladder and the other down in the dumps, the rivalry that had once sparked the fledgling league was, by all appearances, dead. Yet in all likelihood, it will rise again, for of all the teams of the young league, the Los Angeles Galaxy and D.C. United are the only true dynasties. That means that the question isn't *if* they will clash in the future—but *when*.

✴ BY THE NUMBERS ✴

D.C. United versus Los Angeles Galaxy
Regular Season History from 1996 to 2010

Total games played	35
D.C. victories	12
Los Angeles victories	17
Ties	6

✴ MLS CUP CHAMPIONSHIPS ✴

D.C. 4   **Los Angeles** 2

1996, 1997, 1999, 2004   2002, 2005

★ CHAPTER FOUR ★

The Montreal Canadiens versus the Boston Bruins

A grainy black-and-white photograph from April 8, 1952, shows a classic image from National Hockey League (NHL) history. In it, right wing Maurice "Rocket" Richard of the Montreal Canadiens shakes hands with Boston Bruins goalie "Sugar" Jim Henry. A bandage covers a deep gash above Richard's eyebrow. Blood trickles down his cheek. Henry has a black eye.

The picture is a classic because it captures a brief moment of respect between the two fiercely competitive players, adversaries in one of the longest, nastiest rivalries in the league's history: The Montreal Canadiens versus the Boston Bruins.

The Canadiens—or Habs, as they are also

known*—were one of the original teams of the NHL. Founded in 1917 when a previous organization, the National Hockey Association, collapsed, the NHL expanded in 1924 to include teams from the United States. One of those teams was the Boston Bruins, or the Bs, as they are sometimes called.

The rivalry between these squads didn't begin immediately. While the Bruins and the Canadiens met several times in the regular seasons in the early years, they didn't face each other in the playoffs until the 1928–1929 season. That semifinal matchup promised to be an exciting duel. Both teams were the top-ranked squads in their division. The Canadiens had a slight advantage, however, for they had won two of their regular-season meetings; the second was a 3–0 shutout less than three weeks earlier.

But as it turned out, the Bruins handled the

---

*This nickname was born out of a misidentification. The Canadiens' logo is a capital *C* surrounding a smaller capital *H*. According to hockey lore, Tex Rickard, owner of New York's Madison Square Garden, told a reporter in 1924 that the *H* stood for *les habitants*, the French word for *inhabitants*. In fact, the *H* is for "hockey," part of the team's official name: *Club de Hockey Canadien*. No one corrected Rickard's interpretation, however, and in time, *les Habitants* became *the Habs*.

Canadiens without any problems, thanks in large part to their outstanding rookie goalie, Cecil "Tiny" Thompson. Thompson made history that year by becoming the only goalie to earn a shutout in his inaugural game. Now he added two more in the best-of-five series, blanking the Canadiens in Games One and Two while watching his team sneak one into the strings in each of those contests.

Up 2–0 in the series, the Bs needed just one more win to advance to their first Stanley Cup finals. They got it on March 23, a 3–2 victory that had their fans celebrating. And when the Bruins beat the New York Rangers in the finals to win their first Stanley Cup, the celebration grew even more raucous.

Hopes of a Bruins' repeat the following year ran high, and for good reason. The Bs finished the 1929–1930 season with the league's best record of thirty-eight wins, including fourteen in a row, a streak unparalleled until 1982. They logged just five losses and a single tie, the lowest loss-tie tallies ever. Their starting front line of scoring leader Ralph "Cooney" Weiland, Norman "Dutch"

Gainor, and Aubrey "Dit" Clapper was so explosive that its nickname was the Dynamite Line.

Backing them up was one of the most feared and fearless defensemen in the game, Eddie Shore. In the mid-1920s, when the NHL was struggling to make a name for itself, Shore provided the star power needed to get people to take notice. He hit harder, skated faster, and intimidated more than any other player on the ice. He got just as good as he gave, too. "He was bruised, head to toe, after every game," a former teammate remembered. "Everybody was after him. They figured if they could stop Eddie Shore, they could stop the Bruins."

With Tiny Thompson guarding the goal, the Bruins looked unstoppable. Then they faced the Montreal Canadiens.

The Bruins had the Dynamite Line; the Canadiens had the Speedball Line, a front line of Aurèle Joliat, Johnny "Black Cat" Gagnon, and one of the greatest offensive players of the time, Howie Morenz. Small in stature at just five feet nine inches and 165 pounds, Morenz was nevertheless an aggressive scoring machine. That season, he took full advantage of a rule change that allowed forward passing in all three ice zones. In forty-four games, he scored an unbelievable forty goals.

"I would have counted it a full evening had I been able to sit in the stands and watch the Morenz maneuvers," rival Eddie Shore once admitted. "Such an inclination never occurred to me about other stars."

Between the pipes for the Canadiens was standout goalie George Hainsworth. The year before, Hainsworth had logged twenty-two shutouts in forty-four games and ended the regular season with an incredible 0.92 goals-against average. His average was higher the next year because of the scoring rule change, but he was still one of the best net-minders on the ice—as he soon proved.

The 1930 Stanley Cup was a best-of-three series. Montreal stunned Boston the first game, winning 3–0 before the Bruins' hometown crowd. Bruins fans were undoubtedly expecting a victory in Game Two, played in Montreal, for their team hadn't lost back-to-back games the whole season.

But the Canadiens were not to be denied. They scored two goals in the first period, added a third thanks to Morenz in the second, and a fourth soon after that from captain Sylvio Mantha. Eddie Shore scored one for Boston during that same time. Down 4–1, the Bruins came alive in the third, blasting two more past Hainsworth to draw close to a tie.

That was as close as they came, however. Hainsworth held off all onslaughts, and when the final buzzer sounded, the Canadiens had won the Stanley Cup! It was their third franchise championship, their first over the Boston Bruins.

It wouldn't be their last.

Montreal and Boston met four more times in the postseason from 1930 to 1947. In all but the 1943 semifinals, the Habs came out on top, including a four-games-to-one win in the 1946 Stanley Cup. With each passing year, the rivalry between the two teams grew hotter until it reached the boiling point in the 1951–1952 semifinals.

There were two semifinal matchups, one between the Detroit Red Wings and the Toronto Maple Leafs, the other between the Canadiens and the Bruins. Both were best-of-seven series. The Red Wings quickly dispatched the Leafs 4–0 on their way to the Cup finals; the Montreal-Boston contest, on the other hand, went to the seventh game.

The Canadiens destroyed the Bruins in the first two matches 5–1 and 4–0. Boston stormed back to tie it all up at two games each. They each won a third to force the final, deciding game. And what a game!

Playing for the Canadiens was the incredible Maurice "Rocket" Richard. Richard was an intense competitor, a fighter who famously—or infamously—punched officials, leveled opponents, and raced the length of the ice to score seemingly impossible shots. "When he came flying toward you," an opposing goalie once said, "his eyes were all lit up, flashing and gleaming like a pinball machine."

On April 8, 1952, Game Seven of the semifinals, Richard delivered his most impressive goal ever.

That he was even in the game was a miracle. During the second period, Richard collided with Bruin Bill Quackenbush. Richard fell hard. His head smacked the ice—helmets weren't mandatory until after the 1979 season—and he was knocked unconscious. The crowd watched in horror as he was carried off, his body limp and blood dripping from the wound on his head.

The game continued. Each team scored a goal. Going into the third period, the score was tied at one each. That's where it stayed until, to the crowd's amazement and delight, Rocket Richard skated back onto the ice. His head was bandaged, there was blood on his sweater, and he was still dazed from his concussion. And yet, he snared the puck, skated from one end of the ice to the other and—with less than four minutes remaining—flicked in the game-winning goal past Sugar Jim Henry!

Richard was barely aware of what he'd done, however. "I heard the crowd yell, and by that time I was too dizzy to even see," he later confessed. Soon after that goal, he shook hands with Henry—a moment captured forever in that now-famous photograph. While Montreal lost to the Red Wings in the finals, all anyone could talk about was Richard's goal.

Three years later, Rocket Richard headlined the news again, though not for his heroics. On March

13, 1955, during a regular-season game in Boston, Bruin Hal Laycoe slashed Richard's head open with his stick. Enraged, Richard attacked Laycoe with his own stick. Linesman Cliff Thompson tried to break up the fight by pinning Richard's arms behind him. According to one account, Laycoe moved in then and punched Richard. Richard and Thompson slipped and fell. And then Richard punched Thompson.

It was the second time that year he had hit an official. In response, the NHL president, Clarence Campbell, handed down a weighty punishment: "Richard will be suspended from all games both league and playoff for the balance of the current season."

Montreal fans were at first thunderstruck. Then they were furious. With Richard, they had a good shot at the Stanley Cup. Without him, their chances went downhill.

They showed their anger at a home game on March 17, booing Campbell and throwing rotten food at him. The violence escalated when someone tossed a tear-gas bomb near him. As choking smoke filled the Forum, the match was called off and the arena evacuated.

The frenzied fans took their fury into the streets, where thousands of others were already gathered in protest. A riot broke out almost immediately. Angry mobs turned to vandalism, flipping cars, breaking windows, and looting local businesses. Twelve police officers and twenty-five citizens were injured. Finally, Richard got on the radio and pleaded with his fans to stop the madness.

"I still dream about it at night," Richard recalled later in his life.

The Bruins, meanwhile, were having dreams of their own—or rather, nightmares, all of them starring the Habs. Since their last postseason victory over Montreal in 1943, the Bruins had faced the Canadiens in the playoffs six times. All six had ended in Boston defeats, including the team's 1953 bid for the Stanley Cup. The horror continued for the Bruins in 1957 and 1958 when they lost back-to-back championships to the Habs. In all, they had played forty-two postseason games from 1946 to 1958—and lost thirty-two!

The Canadiens, meanwhile, ruled the league in the 1950s. They won five straight Stanley Cups from 1956 to 1960, the most of any team ever in the NHL. They weren't quite as strong in the early 1960s, but from 1965 to 1969, they won four of the five championships played.

Sadly for fans of the Montreal-Boston rivalry, the Bruins faded from the hockey forefront during those same years. They reached the playoffs just twice, in 1968 and 1969. Both times they were eliminated by the Canadiens. Finally, in 1970, they returned to glory and won the Cup. The reason for their surge was a young, energetic defenseman named Bobby Orr.

Orr had joined the Bs in 1966 at age eighteen and earned the Calder Memorial Trophy as Rookie of the Year. One season later, he had added the first of eight James Norris Memorial Trophies, given to the top defenseman, to his awards. In 1970, he added a third Norris—plus the Art Ross, Conn Smythe, and Hart Memorial Trophies. He capped his outstanding year by helping the Bruins win their first Stanley Cup since 1941 with a Game Four overtime goal. (He made photographic history that same moment, for right after the goal he tripped on an opponent's stick and flew horizontally through the air while in midcelebration!)

Also joining in that victory celebration was Phil Esposito, the Bruins' outstanding center. In 1969, Esposito became the first NHL player to reach a hundred points in a season; in the 1970–1971 season, he was first in the league in goals and second in assists. He turned in an amazing performance in the Bruins' postseason, too, scoring thirteen goals in fourteen games, plus fourteen assists. The only thing that would have been sweeter than winning the Cup would have been winning it over the Montreal Canadiens.

But such a victory seemed to be beyond Boston's reach, at least in the 1970s. With a league-best record of 57–14–7, the league's leading scorer, Phil Esposito, and the league's leading assist man, Bobby Orr, the Bruins looked like shoo-ins for a Cup repeat in 1971. Then they came up against a brick wall named Ken Dryden in the quarterfinals.

Dryden, the Habs' rookie goalie, played only six games in the regular season. That he was chosen to guard the crease in the playoffs came as a surprise to many hockey fans. His performance in the series surprised everyone on the Boston team. He started off by blocking all eleven of Esposito's shots in Game One. Esposito was so frustrated with his lack of scoring that after a particularly spectacular save, he slammed his stick against the glass and called Dryden "a thieving giraffe"—a strange insult that perhaps referred to Dryden's imposing six-foot-four-inch, 205-pound stature.

With Esposito all but shut down, the Bruins naturally looked to Bobby Orr. But Orr had his own troubles in the series.

"Stop Orr," Canadien John Ferguson had advised his teammates early on, "and you do stop the Bruins. It's that simple."

The Habs put that advice to work, targeting Orr from the get-go. Dogged at every turn, Orr never found his rhythm. "I want to go, but when I turn it on, I don't go anywhere," he said after the Bruins lost Game Six. He also admitted to being surprised by Dryden, who was "better than we had ever dreamed."

As for Dryden, he knew in Game Seven that the rival team was beat. "They all looked defeated," he commented later. And defeated they were, four games to three. There would be no back-to-back championships for the Bruins. Instead, for the seventeenth time in NHL history, the Canadiens came out on top.

Dryden and the Habs continued to be the thorn in Boston's side throughout the seventies. They faced each other twice more in the finals, in 1977 and 1978. Both times, the Canadiens skated off with the Cup, leading Montreal defenseman Larry Robinson to note, "They will have to spend their summer vacations answering the most depressing question of all: 'Why didn't you win?'"

As upsetting as those losses were, what happened during the 1979 semifinals may go down in Bruins history as their worst moment ever. The Bruins had won their division that year and swept the Pittsburgh Penguins in the quarterfinals to advance to the next round. There, they met Montreal once more. After suffering years of defeat by the Habs, the Bs hit the ice determined to finally rack up a series win over their rivals.

The Canadiens were equally determined to continue their streak over Boston, of course. They rode that determination in the first two games, scuttling their opponents 4–2 and 5–2. But Boston bounced back to take the next two and even the series. Game Five was a decisive 5–1 victory for the Habs—which the Bs answered the next night with a 5–2 win of their own. Once more, the Montreal-Boston series went to Game Seven.

And what a game! The Bruins took an early 3–1 lead, only to see the Canadiens erase the gap and tie it all up. Then, with less than four minutes remaining in the third period, Boston's Rick Middleton netted a goal to give his team the lead!

The teams battled back and forth as the clock ticked down, Boston trying to gain an even greater edge and Montreal fighting to tie it up again. The Bruins were on the attack when their coach, Don Cherry, ordered a line change in the midst of the play.

That would prove to be the biggest mistake of his career.

With just over two and a half minutes left, the players in the box swarmed onto the ice to take their teammates' places when suddenly—*fweet!*—a whistle blew.

Play halted while the officials conferred. Then came the announcement. During the line change, Boston had too many men on the ice! As a penalty, the Bruins had to play shorthanded for two minutes.

"This is a terribly inopportune time for the Bruins to pick up a penalty of that nature," the game's announcer said.

And so it proved to be. During the power play, Canadien Guy Lafleur got the puck. He passed to teammate Jacques Lemaire. Lemaire returned it. Now in scoring range, Lafleur didn't hesitate. With a mighty sweep of his stick, he sent the puck rocketing toward the goal. It bounced off goalie Gilles Gilbert's right shin pad, caught the right pipe—and zinged into the net! Tie game, 4–4!

The game went into overtime. Goalie Ken Dryden was masterly during the extra minutes, throwing himself onto the ice over and over to protect the opening. But his teammates Yvon Lambert and Mario Tremblay made the play of the game. Just nine minutes into the twenty-minute overtime, Tremblay brought the puck down the right side of the rink. Lambert rushed the goal. Tremblay flicked a pass right by the goal mouth. Lambert, barely moving his stick, deflected the pass into the net! With that goal, the Canadiens sent the Bruins packing yet again.

Five years passed before Montreal and Boston

returned to the postseason together. That 1984 series must have struck longtime Bruins fans as a replay of the 1971 Ken Dryden–dominated quarterfinals, only this time, the goalie who confounded the Bruins was named Steve Penney. Like Dryden, Penney had played only a few games for the Canadiens before earning the starter slot in the division semifinals. And as Dryden had done to Phil Esposito, Penney shut down Boston superstar Ray Bourque. Three games later, the top-ranked Bruins were swept out of the postseason.

Boston fell victim to Montreal again in 1985, 1986, and 1987. When the two faced each other in the division finals in 1988, it looked like the same story, different year, for the Canadiens romped over the Bruins 5–2 in the first game.

But then something unexpected happened. The Bruins won the next three games to go up 3–1 in the series. If they could win just one more, they would finally do what they hadn't done since 1943, namely, beat the Canadiens in the postseason.

The fifth match was played in the Forum before a sellout crowd. Boston got on the scoreboard first with a goal by Steve Kasper. Not long afterward,

Bruin superstar Cam Neely swiped the puck away from a Montreal player. Without a teammate in range and a Habs defender close behind, he moved in from the left, cut across the goal, flicked his wrist, and scored over the glove of goalie Patrick Roy.

"Tremendous individual effort to make it two-nothing Boston!" the announcer declared enthusiastically.

Kasper slapped in another goal to make it 3–0. Montreal put one past the Bruins' goalie in the second period and then poured on the pressure with shot after shot on goal. None went in for them, however, and when Neely skated half the length of the ice to deliver yet another goal early in the third, the Bruins had the win!

Boston's general manager summed up the fans' feelings after the victory: "Overjoyed—me and all those people who have been sitting in their living rooms, watching, for all of these years."

While the Bs lost to the Habs in the division finals the following year, the next four postseason meetings belonged to Boston. After 1993, however, the Bruins faded from the forefront. So did the Canadiens. It wasn't until the 2001–2002 play-offs that the rivals clashed sticks again. And when they did, the Bruins' run of victories ended.

The Bruins had finished in first place in the Northeast Division with forty-three wins, twenty-four losses, six ties, and nine overtime/shoot-out losses; the Canadiens' record of 36–31–12–3 had left them in fourth in the same division. But those rankings meant nothing when the teams hit the ice for the conference quarterfinals. After six games, the Habs skated off as the winners.

History repeated itself two years later, when the fourth-place Canadiens overcame a 3–1 game deficit to eliminate the first-place Bruins from contention. The last game was a true nail-biter; going into the third period, neither team had scored. But midway through, Montreal's Richard Zednick took a pass from right wing Alexei Kovalev and scored. He scored again with just eight seconds remaining. "We never gave up," Kovalev said of the come-from-behind victory.

They didn't give up in 2008, either, when the Bruins surged in Game Six to tie the conference quarterfinals at three games each. Instead, the

Habs calmly destroyed the Bs in the deciding game, blanking them while burying five goals into the net for themselves.

That series win marked the twenty-fourth time out of thirty-one meetings that the Canadiens had beaten the Bruins in the postseason. When they faced each other in the conference quarterfinals yet again in 2009, their team's hundredth season, they hoped to make it twenty-five.

Of course, the Bruins were just as eager to post another in their win column. Statistics were on their side, for they had beaten the Habs in five games in the regular season with a sixth ending in a loss. They were the stronger team, too, ranked first in the division; the Habs were eighth in the Western Conference and second in the division.

But as the Bruins knew all too well, statistics don't win games. To come out on top, they needed to hit their rivals with their best play every night.

Bruin Phil Kessel got Game One off to a quick start with a goal in the first period. He ended it with a goal as well, his team's fourth, with just over thirteen seconds remaining in the third period.

The Canadiens, on the other hand, put just two into the net in the 4–2 Boston victory.

The Bruins ran away with the next match, scoring five goals in the first two periods. Two came from the stick of Marc Savard during power plays; Savard also assisted on another goal. Kovalev gave Montreal hope early in the second, scoring just seconds into the period to make it 2–1. But that goal proved to be the Habs' only goal.

The high scoring continued in Game Three—at least for Boston, who put four past the Habs' befuddled goalie. The Canadiens couldn't answer. They netted just two to go down 0–3 in the series.

With the series on the line, Montreal came out fighting in Game Four. Unbelievably, they got on the scoreboard just thirty-nine seconds into the match!

They didn't keep the lead for long. Seventeen minutes later Boston tied it with an unassisted goal by Michael Ryder, who added a personal note to the Habs-Bs rivalry: He had been a Canadien just a year before.

The Bruins sweetened their lead by one before the period ended. The second twenty-minute stretch yielded two more goals, including a second for the night for Ryder. When the Canadiens failed to add any others to their side in the remaining time, Boston skated away with the 4–0 sweep.

"It's definitely a good feeling," Ryder told the press after beating his former teammates on their home ice.

That "good feeling" remained with the Bs throughout their 2009–2010 season. They reached the playoffs again and beat the Buffalo Sabres four games to two to face the Philadelphia Flyers in the next round. That's as far as they got, however, for in a near-epic collapse, the Bs blew a 3–0 lead in the series to be bounced 4–3 from the postseason. The Flyers upended the Canadiens, too, to play against the Chicago Blackhawks, who took the 2010 Stanley Cup.

Fans from Boston and Montreal were disappointed not to see their favorite clubs rekindle their rivalry that season. But they don't need to worry; given the history of these two Original Six teams, there's undoubtedly another on-ice meeting waiting in the wings.

⋆ BY THE NUMBERS ⋆

Montreal Canadiens versus Boston Bruins
Regular Season History from 1924–1925 to 2009–2010

Total games played   705
Montreal victories   339*
Boston victories   257**
Ties   103
Overtime/Shoot-out   6

*333 with overtime/shootout losses
**263 with overtime/shootout wins

⋆ STANLEY CUP CHAMPIONS ⋆

Montreal 24	**Boston** 5
1916, 1924, 1930, 1931, 1944, 1946, 1953, 1956, 1957, 1958, 1959, 1960, 1965, 1966, 1968, 1969, 1971, 1973, 1976, 1977, 1978, 1979, 1986, 1993	1929, 1939, 1941, 1970, 1972

★ CHAPTER FIVE ★

The Chicago Bears versus
the Green Bay Packers

On November 27, 1921, the Green Bay Packers took to the field for the last game of their first professional season. They had done well so far, posting three wins, a loss, and a tie. A big reason for their success lay with their twenty-three-year-old player-coach, Earl "Curly" Lambeau. In fact, Lambeau was the reason there even was a team in Green Bay at all.

Three years earlier, Lambeau had been a starting fullback for legendary coach Knute Rockne's Fighting Irish of Notre Dame in Indiana. But he had to leave school when he came down with a bad case of tonsillitis. He returned to his hometown of Green Bay, Wisconsin, where he accepted a job with the Indian Packing Company.

Working for a company that canned meat put

money in his pocket, but it wasn't his dream job. That position ended up being a stepping-stone for him, however.

Lambeau wanted to play football, but he had no interest in returning to Notre Dame even though it was his best chance to be on a team. Instead, he and his friend George Calhoun, sports editor for Green Bay's local newspaper, persuaded the Indian Packing Company to sponsor a football team. The company agreed to let Lambeau and Calhoun use its field for practices, spent five hundred dollars for uniforms and equipment, and named Lambeau as the team's coach and playing team captain.

The Packers played their first season in 1919 against other area teams from Wisconsin and northern Michigan. They went 10–1, mowing down the competition by incredibly lopsided scores, including one match they won 87–0! Their one loss almost ended in a riot when Green Bay was penalized just as it crossed into the end zone for the tying touchdown. The fans, about two thousand of them, swarmed onto the field in protest, but to no avail. The call stood and Green Bay lost 6–0.

The next year, Lambeau helped his team to a 3–3 tie in their first game with a 31-yard field goal in the final minute of play. He continued to feature prominently in the remaining matches, most of which the Packers won. The Packers were so strong, in fact, that the team made the jump from semipro to professional by joining the American Professional Football Association (APFA), later renamed the National Football League (NFL).

Also in that league was one of the charter members, the Decatur Staleys. The Staleys, named after their founder, businessman A.E. Staley, had been one of the best teams of 1920, going 10–1–2 against teams from nearby Chicago and Minneapolis. Their coach, twenty-five-year-old George Stanley Halas, was also a star player who had helped his University of Illinois team win the Big Ten championship in 1918.

Now, three years later, Halas was facing a momentous decision. Even though the Staleys had a great season in 1920, the Decatur team was losing money. A.E. Staley wanted out and offered to sell the team to Halas. He also suggested that Halas move the team to a much bigger, more sports-oriented city: Chicago. Halas decided that Staley's advice was sound, and so in 1921, the Decatur Staleys became the Chicago Staleys, with Halas as their owner, coach, and starting right end.

The Staleys started off the 1921 season with six wins before suffering a 7–6 loss to the Buffalo All-Americans. Three days after that defeat, they faced the Green Bay Packers for the first time.

The Packers' schedule was light that season, with just six games total. The November 27 match against the Staleys was their last, and they hoped to finish the way they had started, with a win for a record of 4–1–1. The Chicago team was just as eager for victory, of course, and came out fighting.

The game was played at Cubs Park, the field the Staleys shared with the Chicago Cubs baseball team. Three hundred die-hard Packers fans, including members of a brass band, joined local spectators in the stands. Green Bay threatened to score field goals twice in the first quarter. Both kicks were made by Lambeau, but neither was good. The first was short and the second was blocked.

The Staleys didn't score in the first quarter,

either, but in the second, the offense came alive. Right halfback Pete Stinchcomb ran for a 45-yard touchdown. Later, quarterback Pard Pearce danced into the end zone. Going into the half, the score was Chicago 14, Green Bay 0. When Chicago scored again in the final quarter on a pass to Halas from Chick Harley, the Staleys walked away with the 20–0 win.

That decisive victory, while good for the Staleys' record, became memorable for one other reason: It was the first time that Curly Lambeau and George Halas had faced off as coaches in a professional football game. Given that both young men were superb athletes, fierce competitors, and innovative leaders with a shared love of football, one might suppose the two became friends.

In fact, they despised and distrusted each other almost from the start. While the details of how that animosity began are murky, the most likely point seems to center on a player named Heartley "Hunk" Anderson.

Lambeau and Anderson had been on the Fighting Irish football team together at Notre Dame. Anderson was still on that team when he supposedly played—under an alias—for the Packers in the 1921 game against the Staleys. If true, then that was a problem, for the APFA forbade active college players from competing in its league. When one of the Staleys—also a college player bucking the rule—recognized Anderson during the game, he told Coach Halas. Halas told the press, and it was reported in the *Chicago Tribune*.

Until then, the APFA had no trouble turning a blind eye to the illegal use of college players. Now, in the face of such a public accusation, it had no choice but to act. On January 28, 1922, the APFA kicked Green Bay out of the league.

Lambeau lobbied long and hard through the winter and spring to get the franchise back in. He won his appeal on June 24, 1922. Any hope he had of hiring Anderson for his team was gone, however, for by that time Halas had hired Anderson to play for Chicago!

Lambeau was incensed, certain that Halas had gotten Green Bay thrown out of the league so he'd be free to go after Anderson himself. Whether that was true or not, the stage had been set for a hatred that endured for decades afterward.

That hatred is at the core of the rivalry between the Green Bay Packers and the Chicago Bears. Lambeau and Halas openly acknowledged their mutual loathing, and they transferred it to their teams season after season. "If I lost, I wanted to punch Halas in the nose," Lambeau once said. "If he lost, Halas wanted to punch me."

Other factors contributed to the rivalry. The Packers and the Bears (the Chicago club was renamed in 1922, after the Cubs, with whom they shared a field) were in the same division. Competition for the number-one spot in that division—or at least a higher ranking than the other—added ferocity to the feud. So did geography. Only two hundred miles separate Green Bay and Chicago. Like animals that fight to protect their territories, Lambeau's Packers and Halas's Bears battled for supremacy over their turf. Even the makeup of their hometowns set them at odds: Green Bay was a small, rural community, while Chicago was a booming metropolis.

And then there was that fateful November game in 1921, the match that ended with Chicago blanking Green Bay 20–0. As if that drubbing wasn't embarrassing enough, one of the Chicago players, John "Tarzan" Taylor, added injury to insult by punching Packer Howard Buck in the nose!

Three years later, another Packers-Bears slugfest led to the first player ejections. The fight between Green Bay's Walter "Tillie" Voss and Chicago's Frank "Duke" Hanny started with taunts and insults and finished with punches. Lambeau and Halas were still player-coaches then, and Halas made the save of the day by intercepting a Packers pass and nearly running the ball into the end zone for a touchdown when the buzzer sounded to end the game.

Halas and Lambeau faced each other as player-coaches and then as head coaches through 1949. Their dislike and distrust of each other never wavered throughout those years, and neither did their overwhelming desire to beat the other's team. They were rumored to resort to espionage, sabotage, stealing players, and stealing plays to give their team the edge when they next met on the gridiron. They also worked their players harder than at any other time in the season.

"To Halas, that was his number-one game," former Bear Sid Luckman once said.

"We practiced twice on Monday, twice on Tuesday, twice on Wednesday, twice on Thursday, twice on Friday," agreed quarterback Bob Snyder. "We called it 'Green Bay Nut Week.'"

Lambeau's players told the same story. "Before the game, he was wild. During the game, he was wild," recalled Packers tackle Dick Wildung. "He'd lose his cool when he was going to play Halas."

Of the Bears-Packers head-to-head matchups during the Lambeau-Halas years, Chicago came out on top, winning thirty-five to Green Bay's twenty-one, with five ties. The Bears also owned one more championship than the Packers, with seven total since their first in 1921. Remarkably, in one five-year stretch from 1929 to 1933, either the Packers or the Bears were the national champ! That, naturally, fueled their rivalry even more.

Because the Bears and the Packers are in the same division, they will never face off for the top title. In 1941, however, they did meet in the playoffs. The two teams had ended the 1941 regular season with identical records of 10–1, forcing a tiebreaker to determine which would battle the New York Giants for the league title.

The week leading up to this match was a tumultuous one for the nation. On December 7, the Japanese bombed Pearl Harbor; on December 8, President Franklin D. Roosevelt declared war on Japan, bringing the United States into World War II. While the decision to enter the war was extremely popular, it still left people wondering what the future would hold. In the face of that uncertainty, many turned to something familiar to steady themselves.

That may be why forty-three thousand fans packed into Wrigley Field (formerly Cubs Park) on December 14 to watch the Bears-Packers tiebreaker, for they knew they could count on their favorite teams to take their minds off their worries—at least for a while.

Green Bay got on the board first with a sneaky touchdown in the opening quarter. Chicago soon answered but missed the extra point to trail 7–6. The Bears settled down after that and proceeded to demolish the visitors with a field goal and three touchdowns to make it 30–7 at the half. The

Packers managed to reach double digits with a third-quarter touchdown reception, but that was as good as they got. Chicago added another field goal and won 33–14.

The Bears felled the mighty Giants, 37–9, in the championship game a week later to earn their second consecutive NFL trophy. That NFL title, their fifth overall, was doubly rewarding because it tied them with Green Bay.

Behind Halas and Lambeau, Chicago and Green Bay were the powerhouses of the NFL's early decades. But in 1948, Green Bay went into a nosedive, falling near the bottom of the rankings for seven of the next nine seasons. The Bears took full advantage of their rival's struggles by running roughshod over them to a 13–4–1 head-to-head record from 1950 to 1958.

The Packers' troubles finally ended in 1959, when Vince Lombardi took over as Green Bay's coach. A shrewd, hard-nosed fighter, Lombardi not only lifted the Packers out of the cellar, he beat Halas's mighty Bears nearly every time they met. In Lombardi's nine years with Green Bay, the Packers lost just five of eighteen games to the

Bears and finished below them in the rankings just twice, in 1959 and 1963.

In 1963, the top-ranked Bears won their eighth NFL title. The victory brought them even with Green Bay, which had won back-to-back championships in 1961 and 1962. Going into the 1964 season, both teams wanted to be the one to break that tie. To do so, they first had to win their division—and that meant beating the other team in their regular-season meetings.

The first of those meetings came on September 13. Near the end of the second quarter, the score was Green Bay 14, Chicago 3. The Bears had the ball, but they failed to make first down and were forced to punt. Green Bay signaled for a fair catch. Elijah Pitts landed the ball on the Bears' 48-yard line. Then Lombardi called a play that took everyone, including his own players, by surprise. Green Bay was going to try for a free kick.

After a few minutes of confusion, the Packers set up at the line of scrimmage. Quarterback Bart Starr held the ball for kicker Paul Hornung. Hornung connected—and what a blast! The ball split the uprights for three points. The Packers went on to win 23–12.

The Bears learned their lesson well that day, however. Four years later, they beat Green Bay by three thanks to their own "fair catch free kick" play.

These kicks fed the fire of the Bears-Packers rivalry. But they paled in comparison to a kick that occurred on September 7, 1980.

That match took place on Lambeau Field in Green Bay before nearly fifty-five thousand screaming fans. Those screams only increased in volume as the game went on—and when regulation time ended with the score tied at 6–6, forcing the game into sudden-death overtime, the noise was positively deafening.

Green Bay used the extra minutes well, marching down the field to get within field-goal distance with nine minutes remaining. The Packers' chance to unravel the knot lay in their kicker, Chester Marcol. Marcol had booted in two field goals already that day, one from forty-one yards out and the other from forty-six yards. This one was shorter than both, and Marcol approached the challenge with confidence.

But just as Marcol kicked the ball, Chicago's Alan Page leaped up for the block! The ball ricocheted off Page's helmet right into Marcol's face mask. A startled Marcol managed to grab it. And then he began to run, "carrying the ball like a sack of potatoes," according to a Bears player.

On the sidelines, Packers coach Bart Starr was recovering from the shock of the block. When he saw Marcol running, he couldn't believe it. "I was speechless at the time," he remembered. "I was cheering, and chuckling underneath...almost exploding with laughter at what's happening."

What was happening was Marcol was lumbering into the end zone for a game-winning touchdown. "I caught it and I ran. That's all I can say," the delighted kicker said later.

That sudden-death win was one of the few victories Green Bay had over Chicago for the next several years. The Bears walloped the Packers 61–7, the greatest margin in their rivalry's history, in their next outing—and many of the games after that, including an eight-game streak from 1985 to 1988.

As the string of losses grew, so did Green Bay's frustration. That frustration may have led to one of the nastiest tackles in the history of the rivalry.

The hit came on November 23, 1986. Before the game, Green Bay defensive tackle Charles Martin tucked a towel into his waistband. Scrawled on the towel were the uniform numbers of several Chicago players. Martin showed the towel, or his "hit list" as he called it, to several teammates before the game. At the top was number 9, Bears quarterback Jim McMahon.

Chicago was leading 9–3 in the third quarter. The Bears had possession near the 50-yard line. It was third-and-ten. McMahon caught the snap in the shotgun, faded back, and hurled a long bomb. He was watching the play unfold, an interception, to Green Bay's delight, when suddenly— *wham!*—Martin grabbed him from behind and hurled him to the turf!

"Charles Martin took the shot at McMahon well after the ball was thrown," a disgusted television announcer reported. "We expected to see the rough stuff here, but we didn't expect to see something quite that flagrant."

Martin was ejected and suspended for the next two games for tackling McMahon after the ball had been thrown. McMahon had it much worse: He was out for the season with a separated shoulder. But at least the Bears won 12–10.

Green Bay's four-year frustration finally ended November 5, 1989, though that ending was very controversial. With just forty seconds remaining, the score was Chicago 13, Green Bay 7. The Packers lined up on Chicago's 14-yard line for one last play. Quarterback Don Majkowski took the snap and found Sterling Sharpe in the end zone. Touchdown!

Green Bay's celebration was cut short when referees ruled that Majkowski's foot had been over the line of scrimmage when he threw.* Therefore, the touchdown was no good.

The Packers demanded the officials check the instant replay. Four minutes later, the referees reversed their decision: The touchdown was good. When the point after split the uprights, the Packers had the win. Green Bay fans went crazy, and Chicago fans went home feeling robbed. Chicago's coach, Mike Ditka, was so angry over the loss that he insisted that the Bears' print media show the score with an asterisk for years to come.

---

*Soon after this game, the rule for an illegal forward pass was changed. Now, the position of the ball, not the thrower's feet, determines whether the pass is legal. Had that rule been in effect when Majkowski threw the pass, the touchdown wouldn't have counted, for the replay shows that the ball in his hand was over the line of scrimmage.

The instant replay demonstrated the value of film in sports. Six years later, video caught another unbelievable moment in Bears-Packers history— though it didn't take place on the field. On September 11, 1995, a rabid Bears fan leaped from his seat and caught the ball in midair as it fell toward the safety net after an extra-point kick! Unfortunately, his over-the-top show of support didn't help his favorite team. The Bears lost 27–24.

That defeat was the third of ten straight that Chicago suffered at Green Bay's hands. The fourth came on November 12, 1995. The Bears went into the game 6–3; the Packers were 5–4. A Green Bay win would tie the rivals in first place. Those high stakes sparked a shoot-out between Bears quarterback Erik Kramer and Packers quarterback Brett Favre. Favre came out ahead, throwing a career-high five touchdowns in the 35–28 win, despite nursing a painful sprained ankle.

The Packers' winning streak over the Bears finally ended November 7, 1999. The Bears were the emotional favorites because six days earlier, Chicago's legendary running back, Walter Payton, had died of liver cancer. They were ahead 14–13 when the Packers drew within field-goal range on their final play of the game. Green Bay's Ryan Longwell kicked for three. Denied! Chicago's Bryan Robinson had blocked the ball!

"I think Walter Payton picked me up, because I can't jump that high," a teary-eyed Robinson said after the game.

A blocked field goal made the difference for the Bears again on December 22, 2008. Both teams were on fire despite frigid temperatures. With the score tied at 17 and just eighteen seconds remaining, Chicago's Alex Brown batted the ball down one-handed to send the game into overtime. Chicago went on to win 20–17.

Green Bay and Chicago met for the 180th time on September 27, 2010. With equal records of 2–0, they were vying for the number-one slot in the division. They both fought hard, but the day belonged to Chicago, who won 20–17. The Packers had no one to blame but themselves for the loss, for they had a team-record eighteen penalties.

But in the Bears-Packers history, Green Bay has had the most recent—although no doubt not the last—laugh. In 2011, the rivals met in the conference championship game. The Packers won 21–14 to advance to the Super Bowl. They bested the Pittsburgh Steelers 31–25 to earn their thirteenth championship.

Somewhere, Curly Lambeau is smiling.

☆ BY THE NUMBERS ☆

Chicago Bears versus Green Bay Packers
Regular Season History from 1921 to 2011

Total games played	181
Chicago victories	92
Green Bay victories	93
Ties	6

☆ NFL CHAMPIONSHIPS* ☆

Chicago 9	**Green Bay** 13
1921, 1932, 1933, 1940, 1941, 1943, 1946, 1963, 1985	1929, 1930, 1931, 1936, 1939, 1944, 1961, 1962, 1965, 1966, 1967, 1996, 2011

Determining the league champion has changed through the years, as follows: 1920–1932: The NFL champion was the team with the best record, not including ties. 1966–1969: The top team of the NFL played the top team of the AFL (American Football League). These leagues later merged to form the NFL and then split into the National Football Conference (NFC) and the American Football Conference (AFC). 1970–2011: The Super Bowl era of the NFC champs versus the AFC champs.

★ APPENDIX ★

RIVALRY ROUNDUP!
Check out these other great team rivalries!

★ Major League Baseball ★

- The New York Mets versus the Philadelphia Phillies
- The Houston Astros versus the St. Louis Cardinals
- The St. Louis Cardinals versus the Chicago Cubs
- The Cincinnati Reds versus the St. Louis Cardinals
- The San Francisco Giants versus the Los Angeles Dodgers
- The Atlanta Braves versus the New York Mets
- The Los Angeles Angels of Anaheim versus the Los Angeles Dodgers
- The Baltimore Orioles versus the Washington Nationals
- The Chicago White Sox versus the Chicago Cubs
- The New York Yankees versus the New York Mets
- The New York Yankees versus the Los Angeles Dodgers
- The New York Yankees versus the New York (now San Francisco) Giants

✷ National Basketball Association ✷

- The Houston Rockets versus the Los Angeles Lakers
- The Detroit Pistons versus the Chicago Bulls
- The San Antonio Spurs versus the Dallas Mavericks
- The Chicago Bulls versus the Boston Celtics
- The Miami Heat versus the Orlando Magic
- The Miami Heat versus the Cleveland Cavaliers
- The Indiana Pacers versus the New York Knicks
- The Chicago Bulls versus the Los Angeles Lakers

✷ Major League Soccer ✷

- D.C. United versus the New York Red Bulls
- The Chicago Fire versus the FC Dallas
- The Los Angeles Galaxy versus the San Jose Earthquakes
- The San Jose Earthquakes versus the Seattle Sounders
- The Chivas USA versus the Los Angeles Galaxy
- The Colorado Rapids versus the Real Salt Lake
- The FC Dallas versus the Houston Dynamo
- The Columbus Crew versus the Toronto FC

⋆ National Hockey League ⋆

- The Toronto Maple Leafs versus the Montreal Canadiens
- The Calgary Flames versus the Edmonton Oilers
- The Calgary Flames versus the Vancouver Canucks
- The Pittsburgh Penguins versus the Washington Capitals
- The Ottawa Senators versus the Buffalo Sabres
- The Philadelphia Flyers versus the Boston Bruins
- The Chicago Blackhawks versus the Vancouver Canucks
- The Chicago Blackhawks versus the Detroit Red Wings
- The Edmonton Oilers versus the Los Angeles Kings

⋆ National Football League ⋆

- The Miami Dolphins versus the New York Jets
- The Cincinnati Bengals versus the Cleveland Browns
- The St. Louis Rams versus the San Francisco 49ers

- The Green Bay Packers versus the Minnesota Vikings
- The Denver Broncos versus the Oakland Raiders
- The Pittsburgh Steelers versus the Cleveland Browns
- The New York Giants versus the Philadelphia Eagles
- The Kansas City Chiefs versus the Oakland Raiders
- The Dallas Cowboys versus the Washington Redskins

Matt Christopher®

Sports Bio Bookshelf

Kobe Bryant

Dale Earnhardt Sr.

Jeff Gordon

Tony Hawk

Dwight Howard

LeBron James

Derek Jeter

Michael Jordan

Peyton and Eli Manning

Shaquille O'Neal

Albert Pujols

Jackie Robinson

Alex Rodriguez

Babe Ruth

Tiger Woods

Read them all!

Baseball Flyhawk

Baseball Turnaround

The Basket Counts

Body Check

Catch That Pass!

Catcher with a Glass Arm

Center Court Sting

Centerfield Ballhawk

Challenge at Second Base

The Comeback Challenge

Comeback of the Home Run Kid

Cool as Ice

The Diamond Champs

Dirt Bike Racer

Dirt Bike Runaway

Dive Right In

Double Play at Short

Face-Off

Fairway Phenom

Football Double Threat

Football Fugitive

Football Nightmare

The Fox Steals Home

Goalkeeper in Charge

The Great Quarterback Switch

Halfback Attack*

The Hockey Machine

The Home Run Kid Races On

Hook Shot Hero

Hot Shot

Ice Magic

Johnny Long Legs

*Previously published as *Crackerjack Halfback*

Karate Kick

The Kid Who Only Hit Homers

Lacrosse Face-Off

Lacrosse Firestorm

Long-Arm Quarterback

Long Shot for Paul

Look Who's Playing First Base

Miracle at the Plate

Mountain Bike Mania

Nothin' But Net

Out at Second

Penalty Shot

Power Pitcher**

QB Blitz

Return of the Home Run Kid

Run for It

Shoot for the Hoop

Skateboard Renegade

Skateboard Tough

Slam Dunk

Snowboard Champ

Snowboard Maverick

Snowboard Showdown

Soccer Duel

Soccer Halfback

Soccer Hero

Soccer Scoop

Stealing Home

The Submarine Pitch

The Team That Couldn't Lose

Tight End

Top Wing

Touchdown for Tommy

Tough to Tackle

Wingman on Ice

All available in paperback from Little, Brown and Company
**Previously published as *Baseball Pals*